Seventh Revised Edition

Plain English Handbook

A Complete Guide to Good English

J. Martyn Walsh
Anna Kathleen Walsh

McCormick-Mathers Publishing Company
Cincinnati, Ohio 45202

Workbooks to accompany *Plain English Handbook:*

Plain English **1**   *Plain English* **2**

Plain English **3**   *Plain English* **4**

McCormick-Mathers Publishing Company
New York • Cincinnati

Contents

Preface

This is a complete handbook containing all the rules, definitions, and illustrations necessary to mastery of the functional grammar and usage of English.

The treatment of grammar presented here is entirely descriptive. It is based on authoritative studies of the language as it is actually used in the United States, and not on anyone's opinion of what usage should be. Naturally, in view of the scope and purpose of this handbook, the usage presented pertains to standard written usage, except where otherwise noted. The problems of informal speech or colloquial expression are too varied and complex to be contained in a single volume. Insofar as informal discourse should be natural, it is not a subject of instruction. The levels of usage are, of course, clearly explained in this book.

For the more advanced student some indications of recent developments in language study are given in Chapter 8, "Structural Linguistics and Transformational/Generative Grammars," Sections 698 to 748.

The sections are numbered consecutively throughout the book to make effective cross-referencing possible. Numbers in parentheses in the text itself refer to sections in the book.

Sentence Completeness

Effective sentences result from applying many functional elements: good logic, good syntax and grammar, good organization of ideas, careful variation to avoid monotony, and proper emphasis in setting forth important thoughts and images. To a large extent, effectiveness is dependent upon the proper use of modifiers. It is the sentence modifiers that qualify and particularize, giving the sentence the clarity and precision that is the purpose of good writing.

The Sentence and Its Parts

1 A **sentence** is a word or a group of words that expresses and conveys a complete thought from a speaker or writer to a listener or reader. When written, it begins with a capital letter:

   The book is on the table.

2 A sentence must have a **subject** and a **predicate**, either expressed or implied (understood), and it may have an object complement or other complements, modifiers, connectives, and independent elements.

3 The **subject** is that about which something is said:

   Flowers bloom.   *Shakespeare* wrote many great plays.
   Squirrels climb trees.   *Denver* is in Colorado.

4   The predicate is that which is said about the subject:

      Flowers *bloom*.   Shakespeare *wrote many great plays*.
      Squirrels *climb trees*.   Denver *is in Colorado*.

DIAGRAM—Sentence with *simple subject* (13) and *simple predicate* (15):

      Fish swim.

$$\text{fish} \mid \text{swim}$$

5   A sentence must have a subject and a predicate in order to be grammatically complete, but in an **elliptical sentence** (a sentence or clause from which a word or words are properly omitted) either the subject or the predicate or both may not be expressed:

      Subject omitted: (*You*) Read this story.
      Predicate omitted: Who spoke? John (*spoke*).
      Subject and predicate verb omitted: What did I bring? (*I brought*) Books.

6   The receiver of the action denoted by the simple predicate (15) is the **direct object** (sometimes called the **object complement**):

      The carpenter built a *house*.

      The girls picked *corn*.

DIAGRAM—Sentence with *direct object* of a verb:

      Farmers grow *wheat*.

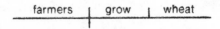

The direct object may be **compound** (17):

      We saw *rocks* and *trees*.

DIAGRAM—Sentence with *compound direct object* of verb:

      Dad planted *shrubs* and *flowers*.

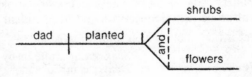

7 A modifier is a word or a group of words that qualifies and characterizes the meaning of another word:

> She ran *quickly*. (*Quickly* modifies *ran*.)
> *The tall blond* man laughed. (*The, tall,* and *blond* modify *man*.)
> The boy *at the desk* is Fred. (*At the desk* modifies *boy*.)
> The girl *whom you saw* is Jane. (*Whom you saw* modifies *girl*.)

DIAGRAM—Sentence with *modifiers* of subject and predicate:

> *The concerned young* woman spoke *frankly*.

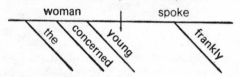

8 A group of related words not having a subject and a predicate is called a phrase:

> The book *on the desk* is a grammar.

9 A group of related words having a subject and a predicate and used as a part of a sentence is called a **clause**:

> Mary is the girl *who swam*. (Subject is *who*; predicate is *swam*.)

10 Although a sentence or a clause must have a subject and a predicate, either can be correct with only one word expressed:

> Go. (sentence)
> The coach said, "Go." (clause)

In both the sentence and the clause above, the omitted subject *you* is clearly understood.

11 **Connectives** (sometimes called **connectors**) serve to join the sentence parts:

> He came *with* me. (preposition, 44)
> Girls *and* boys play tennis. (conjunction, 45)

12 **Independent elements** are expressions that have no grammatical connection with the sentence in which they are found. They are of several kinds:

1. Interjection: *Hurrah!* we won.
2. Direct address: *Ruth,* I want you to help me.
3. Exclamation: *Poor dog!* It needs our help.
4. Parenthetical limiting expresson: He went, *I am sure,* to please us.
5. Responsive: *No,* he has not come.
6. Nominative absolute: *The work being done,* we went home.

Most independent elements are set off from the rest of the sentence by commas (500), whereas the interjection and the exclamation are set apart by an exclamation mark (531).

13   The **simple subject** is the subject taken without any modifier (7)
      A noisy *crowd* gathered immediately.
      The simple subject may consist of more than one word (**compound noun,** 60):
      Betty Ruth Mills is a lawyer.
      The *flour mill* burned down.

14   The **complete subject** is the simple subject with all its modifiers:
      The first game began early.
      The girl at the pool is Evelyn.

15   The **simple predicate** is the predicate taken without any modifier or complement. The simple predicate may consist of more than one word, for it may include a main verb and its helpers (a **verb phrase,** 41):
      The boy *has waited* patiently.
      The book *should have been returned* to the library.

16   The **complete predicate** is the predicate with all its complements and modifiers:
      The girl *has tried patiently.*
      The visitor *has tried repeatedly.*

17   A **compound subject** is one made up of two or more simple subjects:
      Flowers and *trees* are beautiful.

18   A **compound predicate** consists of two or more simple predicates:
      Healthy children *work* and *play.*

19   Both the subject and predicate may be compound:
      Girls and *boys study* and *play.*
      Diagram—Sentence with *compound subject* and *compound predicate:*
      Boys and *girls play* and *sing.*

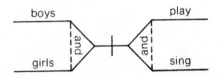

Classification of Sentences

20 Sentences are classified according to their structure or form, as **simple, compound,** and **complex.** (A less common type, the **compound-complex,** is described in section 416.)

21 A **simple sentence** has only one independent clause (397) and no dependent clause (398):

>Our team won the game.

Both the subject and predicate of a simple sentence may be compound (19):

>Mark and Ruth played and sang at the party. (A simple sentence may have any number of phrases—*at the party* is a phrase—but it can not contain a dependent clause.)

22 A **compound sentence** is equivalent to two or more simple sentences (called **independent clauses** when used in a single sentence) connected by **coordinating conjunctions** (367) or by punctuation:

>Joe studies hard and he enjoys school.
>Joe studies hard; he enjoys school.
>Joe studies hard. He enjoys school.

Notice the three ways of writing these words. The last way is not a compound sentence; it is two simple sentences.

23 A **complex sentence** is one that contains but *one* independent clause (397) and one or more dependent clauses (398):

>I was not at home when he came. (The clause *when he came* is dependent.)

♦ Although the definition for the complex sentence given above is the conventional one, there is another type of complex sentence in which the independent clause is not at once evident. In this type a noun clause (400–407) may be an essential element of the independent clause:

>*That she is intelligent* is obvious. (**subject**)
>The truth is *that he forgot.* (**predicate nominative**)
>She said *that she would accept the offer.* (**object**)

24 As to function, sentences are divided into four classes: **declarative, imperative, interrogative,** and **exclamatory.**

25 A **declarative sentence** makes a statement or asserts a fact:

>Our glee club sings well.

26 The **imperative sentence** expresses a command, request, or entreaty:

>Do not walk on the grass. (The subject of an imperative sentence is *you;* it is usually omitted.)

SENTENCE COMPLETENESS

27   The **interrogative sentence** asks a question:

      Where shall we go?   Whom will we meet?   What will we do?

28   The **exclamatory sentence** expresses surprise or a strong emotion:

      What are they up to now!   How beautiful the sunset is!

    A declarative, an interrogative, or an imperative sentence may also become exclamatory when expressed excitedly; therefore, not all grammarians list the exclamatory sentence as a separate class.

29   The **natural or normal order** of the sentence is for the subject to precede the predicate:

      George went to school.

30   When the complete predicate or some part of it precedes the subject, the sentence is in **inverted order:**

      To school went George.

    In an interrogative sentence (27) and in a sentence beginning with the expletive (239) *there* or the adverbs *here* or *there*, the predicate or a part of it usually precedes the subject:

      Have you *received* the book?
      There *are* three books on the desk.
      There your book *will be found.*
      Here *comes* Rose.

31   **END PUNCTUATION** Correct punctuation at the end of a sentence is very important. The declarative sentence (25) ends with a period. The imperative sentence (26) ends with a period. The interrogative sentence (27) closes with a question mark. The exclamatory sentence (28) usually ends with an exclamation mark:

      The trees are most colorful in autumn. (**declarative**)
      Come to see me next winter. (**imperative**)
      Do you like English? (**interrogative**)
      How quiet these forests are! (**exclamatory**)

32   **CAPITALIZATION** Every English sentence (except one in parentheses within another sentence) begins with a capital letter. This is a very important rule.

Writing Good Sentences

33   Do not omit the subject from a declarative sentence:

      Incorrect: Saw you at the show last night.
      Correct: I saw you at the show last night.

    (Subjects are properly omitted from imperative sentences (26).)

34 Do not write a fragment of a sentence as if it were complete:

Incorrect: He studied hard. Hoping to learn it all. (The words *hoping to learn it all* form a phrase which modifies *he*.)

Correct: He studied hard, hoping to learn it all.

Incorrect: Anne had a good time. While she was in the East last summer. (The words *while she was in the East last summer* form a dependent clause used as an adverbial modifier.)

Correct: Anne had a good time while she was in the East last summer.

35 Do not write two or more sentences together as one, without punctuation:

Incorrect: We started early we were eager for the trip.

Correct: We started early. We were eager for the trip.

Correct: We started early; we were eager for the trip.

36 Learn to distinguish a sentence from a fragment and from a group of more than one sentence. An ability to distinguish between a sentence and a group of words which is more or less than a sentence is called **sentence sense.**

While we waited for the train. (This group of words, which resembles a dependent clause, is not a sentence; it is a fragment.)

Men and women running. (Because these words do not have a predicate they do not form a sentence.)

They are running. (This group of words is a sentence. It expresses a complete thought and has both a subject and a predicate.)

Ask your teacher to help you. (This is an imperative sentence. The subject *you* is understood.)

Janice plays basketball she is captain of the team. (Two sentences are incorrectly written as one. This can be corrected in three ways:

1. Janice plays basketball. She is captain of the team.
2. Janice plays basketball; she is captain of the team.
3. Janice plays basketball, and she is captain of the team.)

That was a good game our boys played well were you there? (Three sentences are incorrectly joined as one. This can be corrected: That was a good game. Our boys played well. Were you there?)

37 Do not splice sentences or independent clauses together with a comma:

Incorrect: My brother studies French, he hopes to be a translator. (Two sentences are incorrectly written as one.)

Correct: My brother studies French. He hopes to be a translator.

2

The
Parts of Speech

A DEFINITION, formal and exact, must include all that belongs to the object defined and exclude all that does not; an EXPLANATION, general, may simply throw light upon some point of special difficulty; a DESCRIPTION, pictorial, may include only some general features. In all good writing these three concepts must always be distinguished so that the reader may readily understand the viewpoint of the writer.

Definitions

38 All words may be classified into eight groups called **parts of speech.** The group to which a word belongs is determined by its use in the sentence; therefore, the same word may be any one of several parts of speech, depending upon its use in a given sentence. The eight parts of speech are **noun, pronoun, verb, adjective, adverb, preposition, conjunction,** and **interjection.**

39 **A noun** is the name of a person, place, thing, idea, or quality.

Robert Frost wrote *poems.*   *Ann* lives in *Boston.*
Work brings *satisfaction.*   *People* like *admiration.*

40 **A pronoun** is a word used to take the place of a noun. Through its use, one may avoid repeating name words:

Mary has lost *her* book.   The box has lost *its* handle.
Ruth saw the boys and talked with *them.*

41 A **verb** is a word used to express action, being, or state of being:

> José *painted* a picture.   The law still *exists.*
> That woman *is* a banker.

A verb may be composed of several words, called a **verb phrase:**

> This book *should have been sent* to the storeroom.

42 An **adjective** is used to modify a noun or a pronoun. An adjective may be a single word, a phrase, or a clause:

> We saw *beautiful* valleys and *rugged* mountains. (**single words**)
> The rug *on the floor* is blue. (**adjective phrase**)
> The man *who spoke* is a teacher. (**adjective clause**)

43 An **adverb** is used to modify a verb, an adjective, or another adverb. It may be a single word, a phrase, or a clause:

> He sang *beautifully.* (**single word**)
> The stranger came *into the room.* (**adverbial phrase**)
> Robert left *when I came.* (**adverbial clause**)

In some cases adverbs may modify other parts of speech (316).

44 A **preposition** shows the relation between its object and some other word in the sentence:

> We walked through the woods. (*Through* shows the nature of the relation between *woods,* its object, and *walked,* the verb.)

45 A **conjunction** connects words or groups of words:

> Bob *and* Linda are here.   She came *but* she did not stay.

46 An **interjection** expresses strong feeling: *Ouch! Oh!*

The interjection has no grammatical relation to the rest of the sentence.

47 A **substantive** is any word or group of words that is used as a noun (39) or as a noun equivalent (61).

48 **Inflection** is any change in the spelling or the form of a word to indicate a change in its meaning: *book—books, I—me, has—have.*

> *I have* the *book* here.   He *has* the *books* for *me.*

49 The inflection of nouns and pronouns is called **declension** (144, 159): *man—men, he—him.*

> *He* is a friendly *man.*   The *men* are with *him.*

50 The inflection of adjectives and adverbs is called **comparison** (295-327): *big—bigger—biggest, fast—faster—fastest.*

> The *big* boy ran *fast,* and the *bigger* boy ran *faster,* but the *biggest* boy ran *fastest* of all.

51 The correct arrangement of the inflection of verbs is called **conjugation** (see 205).

52 The use and recorded meaning of a word in a given sentence determines what part of speech it is; therefore, while a word may be one
part of speech in a particular sentence, it may be used as a different
part of speech in another sentence:

> You must not *rock* the boat. (**verb,** 41)
> We saw a *rock* fence. (**adjective,** 42)
> That *rock* is beautiful. (**noun,** 39)
> The word *but* may be almost any part of speech. (**noun,** 39)
> We walked *but* a short distance. (**adverb,** 43)
> All came *but* Ann. (**preposition,** 44)
> We waited for him, *but* he did not come. (**conjunction,** 45)
> They made five yards on the first *down*. (**noun,** 39)
> Karen made a *down* payment on the car. (*adjective,* 42)
> We walked *down* the hill. (**preposition,** 44)
> The old house fell *down*. (**adverb,** 43)
> Adversity will never *down* Bob. (**verb,** 41)

The following are a few examples of the great number of words
that may be commonly used as two or more parts of speech: *while,
right, walk, rain, cry, play, paper, water, call, ground, land, stone,
after, before, fast, outside, iron, last, paint, past, picnic, round, still,
that, fly.*

Your dictionary will record the various meanings that a given word
has developed in the course of its history as a word and will label the
part of speech of its different meanings.

Nouns

53 There are two general classes of nouns: **common** and **proper.**

54 A **common noun** is the name that refers to a class or to anyone of a
class of persons, places, or things:

> The *man* walked down the *street*.   The *cow* is a domestic *animal*.

55 A **proper noun** is the name of a particular person, place, or thing; and
it should be capitalized:

> We are *Americans*.   *Jane* was born in *Alaska*.
> *Apollo 15*, with three astronauts, was launched on July 26, 1971.

♦ Some proper nouns have become the generic or class names of
things and are not capitalized.

> We read about *ohms, volts,* and *amperes* in a book about electricity.
> (from Ohm, Volta, Ampère)

56 In addition to these general classes of nouns there are special classes: abstract, concrete, collective, compound.

♦ The **verbal noun**, though it is not in the strictest sense a pure noun, is very important. (See 61-4, 61-5, 200, 265–268) It has some characteristics of both noun and verb, and it may in form be either an infinitive (199) or a gerund (200):

Writing business letters is important work. (*Writing* is a gerund (200) used as subject of the sentence, but it retains verb force sufficiently to have *letters* as its object.)

To write good letters requires skill. (*To write* is an infinitive (199) used as the subject of the sentence; *letters* is the object of the infinitive.)

57 An **abstract noun** is a noun that names a quality or attribute:

We like *honesty* and *courtesy*.

58 A **concrete noun** is a noun that names something in its material form:

A *telephone* is on the *desk*.

59 A **collective noun** is a noun that is singular in form but names a group or collection (92, 240)

Our *school* has a strong football *team*.

60 A **compound noun** is a noun made up of two or more words. Some compounds are written as separate words, some are hyphenated, and others are written solid as one word: *fountain pen, maple syrup; secretary-general, father-in-law; fireplace, newspaper.*

The only safe guide for determining the correct form of a compound is the dictionary.

♦ Some grammarians classify such nouns as *Duke of Wellington* and *Chase Manhattan Bank* as **phrasal nouns.**

61 There are many **noun equivalents** (substantives, 47), such as the following:

1. **Pronoun** (40): *She* is my teacher.
2. **Adjective** (42): The *young* are full of energy.
3. **Adverb** (43): Since *then* I haven't seen him.
4. **Gerund** (200): *Walking* is good exercise.
5. **Infinitive** (199): *To win* is not our real intention.
6. **Phrase** (8): *Over the top* is our aim.
7. **Clause** (9, 396, 399): *That he has gone* is a fact.
8. **Quotation** (507): *"The time has arrived,"* the speaker said.

62 The modifications of nouns are gender, person, number, and **case.**

63 **Gender** is distinction as to sex; therefore there are logically but two classes of gender. However, the following four are described by many grammarians: masculine, feminine, neuter, common.

64 A noun which denotes a **male** is of the **masculine gender**: *man, boy, father, brother.*

65 A noun which denotes a **female** is of the **feminine gender**: *woman, girl, mother, sister.*

66 A noun which names an object without sex is of the **neuter gender**: *book, rock, desk, house.*

67 Nouns which may denote either male or female or both are said to be of **common gender**: *student, child, singers, teachers.*

68 There are three ways of indicating gender:

    1. Change of word: *man—woman, rooster—hen.*

    2. Addition of a descriptive word: *salesman—saleswoman.*

    3. Use of a suffix: *host–hostess, hero–heroine.*

♦ There is a tendency to avoid making gender distinctions when they are not essential, for example, *host—hostess.*

69 **Person** denotes the speaker, the person or thing spoken to, the person or thing spoken of. There are three classes: **first, second, third.**

    Nouns used alone are always in the third person. When a noun is used in apposition to a pronoun, the pronoun determines the person of the verb.

70 The **first person** denotes the person speaking:

    I, Fred Smith, am willing to go.

71 The **second person** denotes the person or thing spoken to:

    You, Lola, are selected for the honor.

72 The **third person** denotes the person or thing spoken of:

    Our *coach* is here now; *she* will help us.

73 **Number** shows whether the noun refers to one or to more than one person, place, or thing. There are two classes: **singular, plural.**

74 **Singular number** denotes one: *tree, desk, book.*

75 **Plural number** denotes more than one: *trees, desks, books.*

Plurals of Nouns

The dictionary is the only complete guide in forming plurals.

76 Form the plurals of **most nouns** including those **ending in silent e,** by adding *s* to the singular: *bird—birds, tree—trees, tube—tubes.*

77 Form the plurals of nouns **ending in s, ss, x, z, zz, ch, tch, sh** by adding *es* to the singular: *gas—gases, guess—guesses, box—boxes, fez—fezes, buzz—buzzes, church—churches, ditch—ditches, bush—bushes.*

78   Form the plurals of most nouns **ending in o preceded by a consonant** by adding *es* to the singular: *hero—heroes, potato—potatoes*.
Some exceptions to this rule are: *piano—pianos, solo—solos*.

79   Form the plurals of nouns **ending in o preceded by a vowel** (vowels are *a, e, i, o, u*, and sometimes *w* and *y*) by adding *s* to the singular: *radio—radios, trio—trios, two—twos*.
The plurals of a few nouns **ending in o** are formed by adding either *s* or *es* to the singular, but *es* is usually preferred: *volcano—volcanoes—volcanos, zero—zeroes (or zeros)*.

80   Form the plurals of **common nouns ending in y preceded by a consonant** by changing *y* to *i* and adding *es*: *cry—cries, sky—skies*.
Form the plurals of all **proper nouns ending in y** by adding *s*:

   We went to the party with the *Kellys*. Three *Henrys* and two *Marys* were there.

81   Form the plurals of nouns **ending in y preceded by a, e, o, u** by add-only *s*: *day—days, turkey—turkeys, buoy—buoys, guy—guys*.

82   Form the plurals of some nouns **ending in f or fe** by changing the *f* or *fe* to *v* and adding *es*: *sheaf—sheaves, wife—wives, half—halves*.
   Other examples are *calf, elf, leaf, life, self, knife, loaf, thief, shelf, wolf*.

83   Form the plurals of other nouns **ending in f or fe** by adding only *s*: *fife—fifes, roof—roofs*.
   Other examples are *belief, chief, gulf, grief, safe, strife, cliff, proof*.

84   Form the plural of some nouns **by changing vowels** within them: *goose—geese, foot—feet, man—men, woman—women*. Note: *mouse —mice*.

85   Form the plurals of these two nouns by adding *en* or *ren*: *ox—oxen, child—children*.

86   The plurals of **compound nouns** (60) are usually formed by adding *s* or *es* to the main word of the compound; but the plurals of some are formed by adding *s* at the end, and for others the first part of the word is pluralized; in a few cases both words are pluralized: *father-in-law—fathers-in-law, suitcase—suitcases*.

87   Form the plurals of nouns **ending in ful** by adding *s* at the end. Do not make the mistake of placing the *s* before the last syllable.
   She used three *spoonfuls* (not *spoonsful*) of sugar.

88   Form the plurals of letters, symbols, figures, and words regarded as words by adding *'s*, or sometimes just *s*:

Dot your *i*'s, cross your *t*'s, and make your *3*'s (or *3s*) plainer.

You have too many *and*'s (or *ands*) in this sentence.

It happened in the *1890*'s (or *1890s*).

89   Some nouns have the same form in both numbers: *deer, sheep, trout.*

90   Some nouns are plural in form but singular in use: *measles, mumps, ethics, news, summons.*

91   A few nouns are used in the plural only: *scissors, tongs, trousers.*

92   **Collective nouns** are singular when the group is considered a unit, but plural when the individuals are indicated:

The *team* (as a unit) built *its* reputation on honesty.

The *class* (as individuals) have received *their* diplomas.

93   Some foreign words retain their original foreign plurals: *crisis—crises, axis—axes, thesis—theses, cactus—cacti, alumna—alumnae.*

94   The **case** of a noun or pronoun shows its relation to other words in the sentence. There are three cases: **nominative, possessive,** and **objective,** but nouns show case change only in the possessive form. The nominative and objective cases of nouns are used only descriptively now, but these terms help to explain grammatical terms such as *nominative absolute* and *adverbial objective.*

Uses of the Nominative Case

95   The **subject** of a finite verb, that is, one limited by number and person, is in the nominative case:

Mary wrote a book. (A *finite* verb can be used as a predicate, while the *infinite* forms—infinitive, participle, and gerund—cannot be so used.)

96   The **predicate nominative** is in the nominative case:

George is my *friend.*

It was *she.*

She was made *captain.* (289)

A noun or pronoun that completes the meaning of the predicate and denotes the same person or thing as the subject is a **predicate nominative** (sometimes called **subjective complement,** 179-3).

◆ See predicate adjective (179-4, 278, 289).

DIAGRAM—Sentence with a *noun predicate nominative* or *subjective complement:*

The girls were *students.*

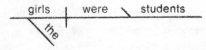

DIAGRAM—Sentence with *compound predicate nominative* or *subjective complement:*

The trees are *cedars* and *maples.*

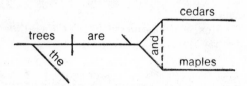

97 A noun of direct address is in the nominative case:

Tom, lend me your book.
Will you help me, *Tom,* with this problem?
When will we finish it, *Tom?*

♦ The noun of address is used to call the attention of the one spoken to. It is separated from the rest of the sentence by a comma or commas (500).

98 A noun used as an **exclamation** is in the nominative case: *Fire! Fire!*

99 The **nominative absolute** is a substantive (47, 61) used in an absolute construction:

The rain having ceased, we went home. (499)
The night being cold, I wore an overcoat.

♦ The absolute construction is a word or a phrase related to the thought of the sentence in which it is found, but not grammatically related to any word of the sentence. It is usually made up of a noun and a participle (201, 269), either with or without modifiers (7). The absolute construction is easily changed into a clause:

The work being completed, we went home.
The work completed, we went home. (*Being* is very frequently omitted in writing.)
When the work was completed, we went home. (clause, 9, 396)

The absolute construction is set off from the rest of the sentence by a comma (499). Never use a period for this purpose:

Incorrect: The work being completed. We went home.
Correct: The work being completed, we went home.

100 A substantive may be in the nominative case by **apposition:**

Ms. Jones, *my teacher,* is in Chicago. (in apposition with the subject)
That is Ms. Jones, *my teacher.* (in apposition with the predicate nominative)

The substantive used in apposition—**appositive**—differs from one used in the predicate nominative (96) in that it has no verb to connect it with the word which it explains. In the two illustrations given, *my teacher* is set off by commas and no verb is used to connect *teacher* with *Ms. Jones*.

DIAGRAM—Sentence with *noun in apposition with the subject*:

Miss Smith, the *teacher*, bought a book.

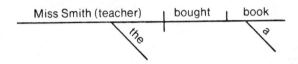

101   An **appositive** is a word, a phrase (393), or a clause (404-407) placed after a substantive (47) to explain it. In 100 the word *teacher* explains who *Ms. Jones* is. The appositive is nearly always in the same case as the word which it explains (but see 118), and it is usually set off by commas (500):

Ms. Jones, my *teacher*, writes books. (**appositive word**)

Mr. Barnes, *driving his car*, met us at the airport. (**appositive phrase**)

The fact *that he is coming* makes us happy. (**appositive clause**)

Although the appositive is thought of usually as a substantive (47), a modifier may be used appositively. The adjective is frequently used appositively (277), just as it is often used in the predicate (278):

The tree, *tall* and *beautiful*, stood near the lake. (*Tall* and *beautiful* are used appositively to explain the kind of tree.)

The tree near the lake was *tall* and *beautiful*. (*Tall* and *beautiful* are used in the predicate, 289, to describe *tree*, and the linking verb *was*, 180, is used as a connective.)

Uses of the Objective Case

102   The **direct object** of a verb is in the objective case:

Richard painted the *picture*.

The direct object is sometimes called the **object complement** (179-1). It completes the predicate by naming the receiver of the action in the active voice (184).

103   The direct object of a verb is also said to be in the **accusative case**, but this term is now infrequently used in English terminology.

104   The **predicate objective**, or **objective complement** (179-2), may follow verbs of *making, naming, calling, choosing, appointing*, and would appear in the position after the **direct object**; the second object completes the meaning of the predicate and relates to the direct object.

We elected Laura *captain.*

105 The **indirect object** is in the objective case:

Mary gave *Alice* a book.

The **indirect object** may be changed into a prepositional phrase, which then follows the direct object:

Mary gave a book to *Alice.*

The preposition (44) used in forming such a phrase is either *to* or *for.*

DIAGRAM—Sentence with *indirect object:*

His mother gave the *boys* some cookies.

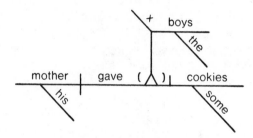

106 The **object of a preposition** is in the objective case:

The great plane flew over the *house.* (object of *over*)

107 The **adverbial objective** is a noun (with its modifiers) used as an adverb:

The child walked *three miles.*   The water was *ankle deep.*

The **adverbial noun** is joined with a preposition to a verb, an adverb, or an adjective to express time, distance, measure, weight, or value. It may be modified by an adjective, such as *three* in the first example.

108 The **subject of an infinitive** (199, 272) is in the objective case:

James believed the *teacher* to be his friend.

There is no need for the *students* to help.

109 The **complement** of the infinitive *to be* having a subject is in the objective case:

James believed the teacher to be his *friend.*

John thought her to be *me.* (272)

When the infinitive *to be* has no subject, the complement is in the nominative case:

Ann wishes to be the *villain* in the play.
He was thought to be *I*. (273)

110 The **direct object of an infinitive** is in the objective case:

Helen likes to paint *pictures*.   The judge tried to help *him*.

111 A substantive may be in the objective case by **apposition** (100, 101):

We admire Dr. Brown, our *physician*.
We heard from Mrs. Hill, our *principal*.

112 The **object of a participle** (201, 269) is in the objective case:

Waving his *hand*, the boy rode away.

113 The **object of a gerund** (200, 266) is in the objective case:

Playing *games* is fun.

114 The **cognate object** is in the objective case:

She ran a good *race*.

When the object of a verb expresses an idea similar to that of the
verb itself, the object is called **cognate**:

He sleeps a peaceful *sleep*.   He fought a good *fight*.

115 The **retained object** is in the objective case:

I was given a *watch* by my father.

A retained object is one that has been retained after a verb has
been changed from active (184) to passive (185) voice:

My father gave (active) me a *watch*. (direct object)
I was given (passive) a *watch* by my father. (retained object)
A watch was given *me* by my father. (retained object)

Note that either the direct or indirect object may be retained.

Uses of the Possessive Case

116 The **possessive case** denotes ownership, possession, or a similar relationship:

This is *Robert's* book.

♦ The possessive case is referred to as the **genitive case** by some grammarians.

117 The noun (or pronoun, 146) in the possessive case is used as a modifier, and as a modifier it is sometimes called a **possessive adjective**
(127, 131, 146, 270, 281):

He found *Sylvia's* book. (*Sylvia's* modifies *book*.)
The *girl's* hair is brown. (*Girl's* modifies *hair*.)

118 A noun in the possessive case may be used as an appositive of another noun (100, 101):

> Bob drives his brother *Harry's* car.

Notice that *brother* would have the possessive form (his *brother's* car) if the appositive were omitted.

119 Ownership or possession may be denoted by the noun in a phrase introduced by *of*:

> the *poems of Keats*   the *music of Schubert*

This is the form most widely used with inanimate things:

> The *leaves of the tree* (instead of the *tree's leaves*) are falling.

But many neuter nouns (66) are correctly used with the regular possessive form, although there is no ownership involved. Here are a few of these: *a week's work, a. dime's worth, for pity's sake, heart's desire, yesterday's report, time's flight.*

Possessive Forms of Nouns

120 To form the possessive singular of a noun, use an apostrophe and *s* after the word (519): the *boy's* cap, the *girl's* book.

It is correct to use either the apostrophe alone or *'s* in forming the possessive singular of a proper noun ending in *s*:

> He did this for *Jesus'* sake.   She carried *Chris's* book.

Form the possessive of a noun of two or more syllables ending in *s* or an *s*-sound and not accented on the last syllable by adding the apostrophe only in written form:

> He did it for his *conscience'* sake.

121 Form the possessive of a plural noun that ends in *s* by adding the apostrophe only:

> The two *boys'* caps are torn.
> The three *students'* books are here.

122 To form the possessive of a plural noun not ending in *s*, add an apostrophe and *s*:

> *men's* shoes, *oxen's* horns

123 In forming the possessive of a compound, place the possessive ending after the last word: *Queen of England's* throne, *sister-in-law's farm.*

The possessives of plurals of compounds (86) are formed in the same way:

> *brothers-in-law's* farms

124 When two nouns are used to indicate common ownership, the sign of possession is placed after the second noun:

Smith and *Brown's* office (Smith and Brown occupy the same office.)

125 When two nouns are used to show separate ownership, add the sign of possession to both nouns:

Opal's and *Edna's* coats are the same color.

126 In such phrases as *nobody else*, the possessive is formed by placing the sign at the end of the phrase:

nobody else's business

127 A noun or pronoun introducing a gerund (200) is usually in the possessive case:

She told us of *Jane's* winning the prize.

He asked me about *my* writing the story.

Pronouns

128 A **pronoun** is a word that substitutes for a noun and that can be used in the same position in the sentence. The classes of pronouns include the following: **personal, relative, interrogative, demonstrative** (138, 281), **indefinite** (139, 281), **possessive** (131). The last three are sometimes called **pronominal adjectives** (131, 140, 281) because they are used as adjectives when the substantive (47) is expressed.

129 The **antecedent** of a pronoun is the word for which the pronoun stands:

Mary brought her book. (*Mary* is the antecedent of *her*.)

The *person* who came here has gone. (The antecedent of *who* is *person*.)

130 A pronoun generally agrees with its antecedent in **gender, person,** and **number.** Its case is determined by its use in a particular group of words. Form modifications of the pronoun are the same as those of the noun: **gender, person, number,** and **case.**

131 An **absolute possessive pronoun** represents the possessor and the thing possessed. It does not modify a noun directly. The absolute possessive pronouns are *mine, yours, his, hers, its, theirs, ours.*

This book is *mine.* (The word *mine* here is equivalent to *my book*; therefore it represents both the possessor and the thing possessed.)

Some authorities classify as **possessive adjectives** (146) the forms *my, your, his, her, its, our, their,* when they are used as modifiers. However, these remain pronouns and agree with their antecedents in gender, person, and number, even when they modify nouns.

132 **Personal pronouns** show by their form whether they are the first, second, or third person (69–72). The simple personal pronouns include *I, you, he, she, it, we, they*, and their inflected forms (144).

133 **Compound personal pronouns** are formed by adding *-self* or *-selves* to some of the simple personal pronouns: *myself, yourself, himself, herself, itself, ourselves, themselves.* (*Hisself* and *theirselves* are incorrect forms.)

134 A compound personal pronoun is used correctly as a **reflexive pronoun** to refer an action to the subject of a sentence:
> He helped himself.

It is also correctly used as an **intensive pronoun** in apposition for emphasis:
> He himself is wrong.

A compound personal pronoun should not be used to take the place of a simple personal pronoun:
> John and *I* (not *myself*) went to the show.

135 A **relative pronoun** is not only a pronoun but also a connecting word. It refers to a substantive (47) in the main clause (397) in which it is found, and it joins an adjective clause (408) to its antecedent. The relative pronoun has a use in the dependent clause (160, 398), such as subject, object of verb, or object of preposition, and it joins the dependent clause to an independent, or main, clause. Because the relative pronoun connects a subordinate clause with a main clause, it is called also a **conjunctive pronoun**. Words used as relative pronouns are *who, whom, whose, which, that*, and *what* (*what* has no antecedent and is equivalent to *that which*):
> The boy *who* sang is here.   *What* was said is well known.

136 The **compound relative pronoun** is formed by adding *-ever* or *-soever* to certain simple relatives. The case of a relative pronoun depends on its use in its own clause:
> We invite *whoever* will come.   (*Whoever* is the subject of *will come.*)

137 The **interrogative pronouns** are *who, whom, whose, which*, and *what*, when they are used in asking questions:
> *Who* is the speaker?

138 The **demonstrative** or **adjective pronouns** (128, 139, 140, 290) point out particular persons, places, or things:
> *This* is my pencil.   *That* is your book.

♦ The most commonly used demonstratives are *this, that, these*, and *those*. When one of these words modifies a substantive (47), it ceases to be a pronoun and becomes an adjective (140, 275, 281, 290):

That is a beautiful tree. (**pronoun**)   *That* tree is beautiful. (**adjective**)

139 **Indefinite pronouns** point out persons, places, or things less specifically than demonstratives do (138):

All did their work.   *Many* were absent today.

♦ Some of the commonly used indefinites are *everybody, everyone, anybody, nobody, each, either, neither, one, none, some, other, another, few, all, many, several,* and *both*. When one of these words modifies a substantive (47), it ceases to be a pronoun (128) and becomes an adjective (140, 275, 281, 290):

Many attended the lecture today. (**pronoun**)
Many students attended the lecture today. (**adjective**)
Some do not like this story. (**pronoun**)
Some students do not like this story. (**adjective**)

140 Words that are sometimes used as adjectives and sometimes as pronouns are often called **pronominal adjectives** or **adjective pronouns** (128, 138, 139, 281):

Several people did their duty.   *Several* did their duty.

141 In using relative pronouns (135), *who* is generally used to refer to persons; *which*, to animals and things; and *that*, to either persons, animals, places, or things:

It was a woman *who* helped us.
The dog, *which* is a faithful animal, is loved by the family.
He spoke of the sailors and the ships *that* were lost.

♦ With clauses that are nonrestrictive or defining, *who* or *which* is used; but with clauses that are restrictive or limiting, *that* is used by careful writers.

142 Make the pronoun agree with its antecedent (129) in number (73):

Each boy should study *his* (not *their*) lesson. (*Boy* is singular and calls for a singular pronoun.)

Case: Forms and Use of Pronouns

143 The case forms of pronouns are always determined by their own use in a sentence, never by the use of their antecedent.

Was it he *whom* they saw? (*Whom* is the object of *saw.*)

144 The nominative case forms of the personal pronouns are *I, we, he, she, they*; the objective case forms are *me, us, him, her, them*. The forms *it* and *you* are used in both the nominative and objective case. *Her* may be either objective or possessive.

Declension of Personal Pronouns

| | SINGULAR | | | PLURAL | | |
--------	Nomina-tive	Possessive	Objec-tive	Nomina-tive	Possessive	Objec-tive
1ST PER.	I	my, mine	me	we	our, ours	us
2ND PER.	you	your, yours	you	you	your, yours	you
3RD PER.	he	his	him	they	their, theirs	them
	she	her, hers	her	they	their, theirs	them
	it	its	it	they	their, theirs	them

145 Personal pronouns (132) in the nominative case have the same uses as nouns (95–101), as follows:

1. Subject of a verb: *I* went home.
2. Predicate nominative: I am *he.*
3. Direct address: *You*, Fred, can give a demonstration.
4. Exclamation: Lucky *you!*
5. Nominative absolute: *He* being ill, we did not go.
6. Appositive: We, Mary and *I*, played ball.
7. Complement of the infinitive *to be* not having a subject: John was thought to be *I.* (See 109, 274.)

146 Personal pronouns (132) in the possessive case **do not require the sign of possession as do nouns.** The possessive forms (see 131, 144) are *my, mine, our, ours, his, her, hers, their, theirs, its, your, yours:*

The bird sang *its* (not *it's*) song.

The only correct use of the apostrophe with the personal pronoun is in contractions which are often found in reported speech, but less frequently in formal written text.

It's time to go home.   They're ready to see you.

The following pronouns in the possessive case are sometimes called **possessive adjectives:** *my, your, his, her, its, our, their.* (131, 281)

147 Personal pronouns in the **objective case** (144) may be used in these ways:

1. Direct object of a verb: The teacher praised *her.*
2. Indirect object: He gave *her* a copy of the essay.
3. Object of a preposition: I spoke to *him.*
4. Subject of an infinitive: He asked *me* to stay.
5. Complement of the infinitive *to be* having a subject: Did you think Sally to be *her?* (109, 273)
6. Object of a participle: Seeing *me* at the door, my aunt smiled happily.
7. Object of an infinitive: Mary tried to help *me.* (110)

8. **Object of a gerund:** Helping *him* was my duty. (113, 200, 266)

9. **Appositive:** Ann invited us, Bill and *me*.

148 A noun or pronoun following *than* or *as* is in the nominative or objective case according to its construction in the elliptical (5) clause to which it refers:

You are stronger than *he* (is strong).

You like her better than (you like) *me*.

Tony is not as strong as *you* (are strong).

Tony likes him as well as *you* (do).

149 When a subject or a predicate nominative is compound (17, 96), both parts should be in the nominative case form:

John and *he* are going.

The winners are Bill and *she*.

150 Do not repeat a subject by using a pronoun after it:

Charles (not *Charles he*) studied hard.

151 When a pronoun is used as the subject or as a predicate nominative and has a noun in apposition (100, 101) following it, the nominative form (144) of the pronoun should be used:

All *we* students went to the play.

It was *we* girls who did the work.

152 A personal pronoun used as a **predicate nominative** should be in nominative case form (144, 180):

The guests were *she* (not *her*) and *they* (not *them*).

♦ Some authorities feel that "It is *me*" is natural and acceptable in colloquial speech, but careful writers prefer "It is *I*" in formal written work.

153 If a pronoun appears in the **compound object** of a **verb** or of a **preposition**, the pronoun should be in the objective case form:

Our uncle saw Clyde and *me*.   The woman spoke to Grace and *me*.

154 When the **indirect object** (105) is compound, all pronoun parts should be in the objective case form:

The farmer gave *her* and *me* some apples.

155 When a pronoun is the direct (147-1) or the indirect (147-2) object of a verb and has a noun in apposition (101), use the objective form of the pronoun:

Our teacher saw *us* girls.   Bob sent *us* boys a message.

156 *But*, when used in the sense of *except*, is a preposition (341) and must, like *except* and *between*, have an object:

I invited all the girls but *her*.   He stood between you and *me*.

157 When a pronoun is the object of a preposition (147-3) and has with it a noun in apposition (101), use the objective form of the pronoun:

Sue came with *us* students.

158 *Who, whom, whose, which,* and *what* are **interrogative pronouns** when they are used in asking questions.

159 *Who,* whether interrogative or relative, is the nominative case form:

Who did Wilma say was the speaker? (*Who* is the subject of *was;* the clause *who was the speaker* is the object of *say.*)

Whom is the objective case form:

Whom will you send to town?
I met the girl of *whom* you spoke. (relative)

Declension of Relative Pronouns

SINGULAR AND PLURAL

Nominative	Possessive	Objective
who	whose	whom
which	whose	which

160 The case form of the pronoun used as a relative (135) depends upon the use of the relative in the clause (9) it introduces:

This is the boy *who* lost his book. (*Who* is subject of *lost.*)
The man *whom* you saw is my friend. (*Whom* is object of *saw.*)

161 The compound relative *whoever* is the nominative case form:

Stop *whoever* comes this way. (*Whoever* is the subject of *comes.* The clause *whoever comes this way* is the object of *stop.*)

162 The compound relative *whomever* is the objective case form:

Send it to *whomever* you choose. (*Whomever* is the object of *choose.* The clause *whomever you choose* is the object of the preposition *to.*)

Whomever you ask will be invited. (*Whomever* is the object of *ask.* The clause *whomever you ask* is the subject of the verb *will be invited.*)

♦ The case forms of the compound relative *whoever* seem more easily confused than the forms of *who.* When the compound relatives are used, the form may be determined more readily if words are supplied to show an antecedent. In 161, for example, the sentence would be expanded to *You stop him who comes this way.* The example in this section would be *He whom you ask will be invited.*

Number

163 The **indefinite pronouns** *each, either, neither, one, everyone, anyone, someone, no one, nobody, anybody, somebody, everybody* are singular (242):

Each girl should do *her* best.   Neither boy could sing *his* song.

26   THE PARTS OF SPEECH

Sometimes the meaning is so clearly plural that a singular personal pronoun cannot be used to refer to the indefinite pronoun:

Everyone was so busy writing a version of the story that *they* did not notice who had come in. (Not *he* did not notice.)

♦ Current informal usage permits use of the plural with various indefinite pronouns.

164 A pronoun must be singular when it refers to a noun modified by such indefinite adjectives (139, 140) as *each, every,* and *neither*:

Each boy brought *his* ticket.   Every girl brought *her* books.

165 A pronoun that refers to a collective noun (59) is singular if the group acts as a unit:

The band has won fame because of *its* leader.

But the pronoun is plural if the individuals of the group act as individuals:

The band have ordered *their* new instruments.

Usage

166 Most experts agree that *which* should not be used to refer to a complete statement (376):

Questionable: He had to work, *which* caused him to be late.
Better: He was late *because* he had to work.

167 The word *same* should not be used as a pronoun instead of *it* or *them*:

I have read your offer (offers) and have decided to accept *it* (*them*) (not *same* or *the same*).

168 *Them* is never used as an adjective nor as the subject of a sentence:

Those (not *Them* or *Them there*) books are mine.

169 *They* should not be used with indefinite reference:

People (not *They*) say that he is talented.

Verbs

170 A verb (41) is a word that expresses action, being, or state of being. (A verb may be formed by a group of words; such a group is called a **verb phrase** or a **phrasal verb** (181, 391.) According to the way in which they form their principal parts (202), verbs are divided into two classes: **regular** (weak) and **irregular** (strong).

171 A **regular** (weak) **verb** forms its past tense (193) and past participle

(201) by adding *d*, *ed*, or *t* to the present tense (191): *hear—heard—heard, help—helped—helped, deal—dealt—dealt.*

172 An **irregular** (strong) **verb** usually forms its past tense and past participle by changing a vowel of the present (or infinitive, 199) form: *begin—began—begun.*

Sometimes a different word may be used for a principal part: *go—went—gone.*

Sometimes all the principal parts are the same: *set—set—set.*

Transitive and Intransitive

173 According to use, verbs are classified as **transitive** or **intransitive.**

174 A **transitive verb** has a receiver of the action expressed in the meaning of the verb to complete the meaning. When the actor is the subject (3), the receiver of the action is the object (6):

Bob *wrote* a letter.

When the receiver of the action is the subject, the verb is in the passive voice (185) but remains transitive:

A letter *was written* by Bob.

The verb *was written* is in the passive voice. When the subject is the receiver of the action, the name of the actor may not be expressed:

Many letters *were written.*

175 An **intransitive verb** does not require a receiver of the action expressed in the meaning of the verb:

The eagle *flew* over the mountain.

176 Many verbs may be used as transitive in one sentence and as intransitive in another sentence:

She sings well. (intransitive)

She sings beautiful songs. (transitive)

177 Intransitive verbs are of two classes: **complete** and **linking.**

178 A **complete verb** is an intransitive verb which makes a meaningful statement without the help of any other word:

Birds *fly.*   Fish *swim.*   The horse *drinks.*   Children *play.*

179 A verb sometimes requires a substantive (47) or an adjective (42, 275) to complete its meaning. The substantive or adjective added is called a **complement.** There are several classes of complements:

1. **Direct object** (102) or object complement:

Bob caught the *ball.*   Many won the *trophy.*

2. **Predicate objective** (104) or objective complement:

They elected her *captain.*   We appointed him *leader.*

3. **Predicate nominative** (96) or subjective complement:

Browning was a great *poet*.   The woman became a *writer*.

4. **Predicate adjective** (289). The predicate adjective completes the predicate of the sentence and modifies, describes, or points out the subject of the sentence:

The roses are *beautiful*. (The predicate adjective *beautiful* completes the linking verb *are* and describes the subject *roses*.) (180)

The apple looks *good*. (289)

DIAGRAM—Sentence with *predicate adjective*:

The old woman was very *sad*.

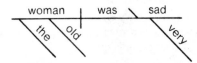

180 **A linking verb,** sometimes called a **copulative verb,** is an intransitive verb that connects the subject with a predicate substantive (47) or a predicate adjective (289). The substantive or adjective following the linking verb either means the same as the subject or describes, limits, or points out the subject:

Webster *was* a statesman.   The rose *is* beautiful.

The most commonly used linking verb is *be* in its various forms such as *am, is, was, were*. Some other verbs used as linking verbs are *seem, become, appear, prove, look, remain, feel, taste, smell, sound, turn, grow, stay, continue*.

A noun or pronoun joined to a subject by a linking verb is in the nominative case (96, 145-2, 152):

It is *he*.   That was *she*.

Auxiliary Verbs

181 **An auxiliary verb** is a verb that aids or helps another verb express various shades of meaning. A verb with its helper or helpers is a **verb phrase** (41, 391). Some verbs used as auxiliaries are *do (did), be (am, is, are, was, were), have (has, had), may (might), can (could), must, will, shall (would, should)*. Some of these verbs serve not only as auxiliaries but also as main verbs:

Jack *did* bring his book. (**auxiliary**)

Jack *did* good work. (**main verb**)

182 Although the linking verb *be* (180) **does not take an object,** all the forms of this verb may become auxiliaries in transitive verb phrases (174):

It *is* she. (linking)

Ruth *is* writing a letter. (*Is* is an **auxiliary** used in forming the verb phrase *is writing*; *write* is a transitive verb with the object *letter*.)

The forms of *be* are used also as auxiliaries in forming the passive voice (185).

The house *was* destroyed by fire.

The report *has been* received.

183 The modifications of a verb indicate its **voice, mood, tense, person,** and **number.**

Voice

184 The **voice** of a verb indicates whether the subject of the verb acts or is acted upon. **Active voice** denotes that the subject of the verb is the actor:

The man *called* the dog.

185 **Passive voice** denotes that the subject receives the action:

The dog *was called* by the man.

The passive is always a verb phrase (41, 181, 391) composed of a form of the auxiliary (181, 208) *be* followed by a past participle (201, 208):

The letter *has been written* by the manager.

♦ Passive verbs sometimes have two receivers of the action: the subject and the retained object (115):

She was given a *scholarship*.

Mood

186 **Mood** (or **mode**) indicates the manner in which the action is conceived.

187 The **indicative mood** makes a statement of fact or asks a question:

He *is* my friend.   *Is* she a teacher?

188 The **imperative mood** gives a command or makes a request:

Shut the door.

Will you please *return* the book. (Note that a question mark is not used.)

189 The **subjunctive mood** expresses a doubt, a wish, a prayer, or a condition contrary to fact:

I wonder if it *be* true.   Peace *be* with you!

I wish I *were* a lawyer.   If I *were* you, I should go.

The **present subjunctive** occurs after verbs like *demand* (259):
I insist that he *go*.

Tense

190 **Tense** denotes the time of the action indicated by a verb. The time is not always the same as that indicated by the name of the tense.

191 The **present tense** may express action which is going on at the present time or which occurs always, repeatedly, or habitually:
The boys *are* ready to leave now.
They *go* by bus to school.
She *eats* cereal for breakfast.

The present tense may express future time:
The train *leaves* in five minutes.

It may be used as an historical present, referring to an event completed in past time.
The detective *solves* the mystery just in time.

192 The **present perfect tense** expresses action completed at the present time or continuing into the present:
He *has written* a letter to his uncle. (**completed**)
I *have lived* here for many years. (**continuing**)

193 The **past tense** expresses action completed at a definite time in the past:
He *wrote* the letter yesterday.

Do not use the emphatic past tense for the present perfect:
Joe *has* (not *did*) not come yet.

194 The **past perfect tense** expresses action completed before a stated or known time in the past:
He *had written* the letter before I saw him.

195 The **future tense** expresses action which will take place in the future:
He *will write* the letter tomorrow.

196 The **future perfect tense** expresses action which will be completed before a stated or known time in the future:
He *will have written* the letter before we arrive tomorrow.

197 A verb as a rule agrees with its subject in person (69–72) and number (73–75). Failure to observe this rule causes many errors:
He *doesn't* (not *don't*) know what to do.

♦ See 236–249, 262, and other sections under "verb, agreement of verb and subject" in the Index.

The Verbals

198 There are three forms of the verb, called **verbals, that are also used as** other parts of speech: **infinitive, gerund, and participle.**

199 The **infinitive** (265) is the form of the verb usually preceded by *to* (see 232)—a function word used to indicate that the following word is an infinitive.

We like *to play* basketball.

The **present infinitive** is the same as the simple present-tense form of the verb, usually preceded by *to: to see, to go, to do.*

The **perfect infinitive** is formed by placing *to have* before the past participle (201): *to have seen, to have gone, to have done.*

200 The **gerund** (56, 266–268) is a **verbal noun** (56) ending in *ing*. The gerund may, like any verb, take an object and it may be modified by an adjective or an adverb. A gerund is sometimes referred to as a **participial noun,** as in reality it is a participle used as a noun. The gerund is the name of an action:

Trying is commendable. (*Trying* is the subject of the sentence.)

Don enjoys *reading* history. (*Reading* is the object of the verb *enjoys* and it has its own object *history.*)

Walking rapidly is good exercise. (The adverb *rapidly* modifies the gerund *walking.*)

201 A **participle** is a verbal (198) which has some of the properties of a verb and some of the properties of an adjective. It is used, as an adjective, to modify a noun or a pronoun; it may, as a verb, take an object:

The person *waving* the flag is Robert. (*Waving* modifies *person* as an adjective and takes an object *flag* as a verb.)

The **present participle** ends in *ing* and generally describes an action going on at the same time as some other action, but it sometimes refers to time preceding that of the verb used as predicate:

Sitting here, we see the parade.

Standing at the window, I saw the parade.

The present participle is used in progressive forms of the active voice (205 and 209).

The **past participle** generally indicates completed action.

The past participle of a regular verb (171) usually has the same form as the past tense (193), but the form of the past participle of the irregular verbs (172) show numerous changes in form (204).

This was a work *done* for others.

The terms *suggested* by the committee were fair.

The past participle form is always combined with *have, has,* and *had* to form the perfect tenses (192, 194, 196).

The **perfect participle** is formed of *having* and the past particple:

Having finished the work, the people went home.

Principal Parts

202 The principal parts of a verb are the first person (70) singular (74) of the present (191) indicative (187), the first person singular of the past (193) indicative, and the past participle (201):

I go—I *went*—I have *gone.*   I *see*—I *saw*—I have *seen.*

203 Do not confuse the principal parts of irregular verbs (172):

I *saw* (not *seen*) him yesterday.

204 PRINCIPAL PARTS OF THE IRREGULAR VERBS

The reference list that follows presents the variations in form that speakers and writers of English today will need to recognize; included in the list are some verbs of quite limited present use, but they have been included for their recognition as irregular forms. Whenever more than one form is shown, the first is the more commonly used. The numbered notes will indicate special uses or limitations in use; they are keyed to the list for reference.

PRESENT TENSE	PAST TENSE	PAST PARTICIPLE
abide	abided, abode	abode
—	—	accursed,[2] accurst
arise	arose	arisen
awake	awoke	awoke
be (am, is)	was, were	been
bear (*bring forth*)	bore	born [3]
bear (*carry*)	bore	borne
beat	beat	beaten, beat
beget	begot	begotten
begin	began	begun
behold	beheld	beheld, beholden [1]
bend	bent	bent
bereave	bereaved, bereft	bereaved,[1] bereft
beseech	beseeched, besought	besought
bespeak	bespoke	bespoken
bet	bet, betted	bet
bid (*command*)	bade	bid
bid (*money*)	bid	bidden, bid
bind	bound	bound, bounden [1]
bite	bit	bit, bitten
bleed	bled	bled
blend	blended, blent	blended, blent

PRESENT TENSE	PAST TENSE	PAST PARTICIPLE
bless	blessed, blest	blessed,[2] blest
blow	blew	blown
break	broke	broken
breed	bred	bred
bring	brought	brought
build	built, builded	built, builded
burn	burned, burnt	burned, burnt
burst	burst	burst, bursted [1]
buy	bought	bought
cast	cast	cast
catch	caught	caught
chide	chided, chidden	chided, chidden
choose	chose	chosen
cleave (*split*)	clove, cleft	cloven,[1] cleft
cleave (*adhere*)	cleaved, clave [4]	cleaved
cling	clung	clung
clothe	clothed, clad	clothed, clad
come	came	come
cost	cost	cost
creep	crept	crept
crow	crowed, crew	crowed, crown [4]
curse	cursed	cursed, cursed [2]
cut	cut	cut
deal	dealt	dealt
dig	dug	dug
dip	dipped	dipped
dive	dived, dove	dived
do	did	done
draw	drew	drawn
dream	dreamed, dreamt	dreamed, dreamt
dress	dressed, drest	dressed, drest
drink	drank	drunk, drunken [1]
drive	drove	driven
drop	dropped	dropped
dwell	dwelt, dwelled	dwelt, dwelled
eat	ate	eaten
engrave	engraved	engraved, engraven [4]
fall	fell	fallen
feed	fed	fed
feel	felt	felt
fight	fought	fought
find	found	found
flee, fly	fled	fled
fling	flung	flung
fly	flew	flown
forbear	forbore	forborne

PRESENT TENSE	PAST TENSE	PAST PARTICIPLE
forbid	forbade, forbad	forbidden, forbid
forget	forgot	forgot, forgotten
forsake	forsook	forsaken
freeze	froze	frozen
freight	freighted	freighted, fraught [1]
get	got	got, gotten [6]
gild	gilded	gilded
gird	girded, girt	girded, girt
give	gave	given
go	went	gone
grave	graved	graved, graven [1]
grind	ground	ground
grow	grew	grown
hang (*suspend*)	hung, hanged	hung
hang (*execute*)	hanged, hung	hanged
have	had	had
hear	heard	heard
heave	heaved, hove [7]	heaved, hove
hew	hewed	hewn, hewed
hide	hid	hidden, hid
hit	hit	hit
hold	held	held
hurt	hurt	hurt
keep	kept	kept
kneel	knelt	knelt
knit	knitted, knit	knitted, knit
know	knew	known
lade [4]	laded	laden,[1] laded
lay	laid	laid
lead	led	led
lean	leaned, leant	leaned, leant
leap	leaped	leaped, leapt
learn	learned, learnt [8]	learned, learnt
leave	left	left
lend	lent	lent
let	let	let
lie (*position*)	lay	lain, lorn [1]
lie (*tell a falsehood*)	lied	lied
light (*set fire to*)	lighted, lit	lighted, lit
light (*descend*)	lighted, lit	lighted, lit
load	loaded	loaded, laden [1]
lose	lost	lost
make	made	made
mean	meant	meant
meet	met	met
melt	melted	melted, molten [1]
mow	mowed	mowed, mown

PRESENT TENSE	PAST TENSE	PAST PARTICIPLE
owe	owed, ought [4]	owed
—	ought [5]	own [5]
pay	paid	paid
pen (confine)	penned	penned, pent [1]
plead	pleaded, plead	pleaded, plead
prove	proved	proved, proven [1]
put	put	put
quit	quit, quitted	quit, quitted
read	read	read
rend	rent	rent
rid	rid, ridden	rid, ridden
ride	rode	ridden
ring	rang	rung
rise	rose	risen
roast	roasted	roasted, roast [1]
run	ran	run
saw	sawed	sawed, sawn
say	said	said
see	saw	seen
seek	sought	sought
seethe	seethed, sod [4]	seethed, sod,[4] sodden [1]
sell	sold	sold
send	sent	sent
sew	sewed	sewed, sewn
shake	shook	shaken
shape	shaped	shaped, shapen [1]
shave	shaved	shaved, shaven [1]
shear	sheared, shore	sheared, shorn
shed	shedded	shed
shine	shone	shone
shoe	shod	shod
shoot	shot	shot
show	showed	shown, showed
shred	shredded, shred	shredded, shred
shrink	shrank, shrunk	shrunk, shrunken
shrive	shrived	shrived, shriven
shut	shut	shut
sing	sang, sung	sung
sink	sank, sunk	sunk, sunken [1]
sit	sat	sat
slay	slew	slain
sleep	slept	slept
slide	slid	slid, slidden
sling	slung	slung

PRESENT TENSE	PAST TENSE	PAST PARTICIPLE
slink	slunk	slunk
slit	slit	slit
smell	smelled, smelt	smelled, smelt
smite	smote	smitten
sow	sowed	sown, sowed
speak	spoke	spoken
speed	sped	sped
speed	speeded	speeded
spell	spelled, spelt	spelled, spelt
spill	spilled, spilt	spilled, spilt
spin	spun, span	spun
spit	**spat, spit**	spat, **spit**
split	split	split
spoil	spoiled, spoilt	spoiled, spoilt
spread	spread	spread
spring	sprang	sprung
stand	stood	stood
stay	stayed, staid	stayed, staid
stave	staved, stove	staved, stove
steal	stole	stolen
stick	stuck	stuck
stink	stank, stunk	stunk
strew	strewed	strewed, strewn
stride	strode	stridden
strike	struck	struck, stricken [1]
string	strung	strung
strive	strove	striven
sting	stung	stung
swear	swore	sworn
sweat	sweat, sweated	sweat, sweated
sweep	swept	swept
swell	swelled	swelled, swollen
swim	swam	swum
swing	swung	swung
take	took	taken
teach	taught	taught
tear	tore	torn
tell	told	told
think	thought	thought
thrive	thrived, throve	thrived, thriven
throw	threw	thrown
thrust	thrust	thrust
toss	tossed, tost	tossed, tost
tread	trod	trodden, trod
wake	woke, waked	woke, waked, woken
wash	washed	washed, washen [4]
wax (*grow*)	waxed	waxed
wear	wore	worn

PRESENT TENSE	PAST TENSE	PAST PARTICIPLE
weave	wove	woven, weaved
wed	wed, wedded	wed, wedded
weep	wept	wept
wet	wet, wetted	wet, wetted
win	won	won
wind (*twist*)	wound	wound
wind (*sound*)	wound	wound, winded
(won) [4] (*accustomed*)	—	wont,[1] wonted [1]
wont [4] (*need to*)	wonted, wont	—
work	worked, wrought	worked, wrought
wring	wrung	wrung
write	wrote	written
writhe	writhed	writhed, writhen [4]

[1] The following participles are now used only as adjectives: I am *beholden* to you; the *bereaved* father; his *bounden* duty; a *bursted* bubble; a *cloven* foot; *fraught* with danger; a *graven* image; a *drunken* driver; heavily *laden* ships; now used only in *forlorn*; *molten* gold; *pent*-up anger; a *proven* case; *roast* beef; ill-*shapen*; a clean *shaven* face; a *sodden* meadow; a *sunken* garden; *stricken* by disease; *wont* to act with spirit (rare); in his *wonted* style (rare).

[2] Used as in [1] above, but notice the shift in word stress in their pronunciation as adjectives: *accurséd, curséd, blesséd, belovéd, learnéd*.

[3] Now used only in phrases such as: *born* into this world; *born* in bondage.

[4] Obsolete or archaic and no longer in use: *clave, engraven, lade, ought* (as the past tense of *owe*); *washen*; *writhen*; *won* and *wont* (as the present tense); *crown, sod*.

[5] *Ought* is an old past form of *owe*, replaced now by *owed*; *ought* is now used in a present sense, you *ought* to do it. *Own* is now used as an adjective, his *own* book.

[6] *Got* is the regular past form, with *got* or *gotten* as the past participle in standard English. In formal writing, *got* is preferred in the meaning of *possess* or *have*. In spoken English, *got* and *gotten* are equally used in the sense of *acquire* or *become*.

[7] Said principally of ships; the vessel *hove* in sight.

[8] A number of verbs show two past forms, one in *-ed*, the other in *-t*, as in *learned, learnt*. In writing, the *-ed* form is preferred, while in speaking the *-t* form is very widely heard.

Conjugation

205 The conjugation of a verb is the orderly arrangement of its forms through its voices (184–185), moods (186–189), tenses (190–196), persons (69–72, 197), and numbers (73–75, 197).

206 CONJUGATION OF THE VERB BE

INDICATIVE MOOD		Singular	Plural
Present Tense		1. I am 2. you are 3. he is	1. we are 2. you are 3. they are
Past Tense		1. I was 2. you were 3. he was	1. we were 2. you were 3. they were
Future Tense		1. I shall be 2. you will be 3. he will be	1. we shall be 2. you will be 3. they will be
Present Perfect Tense		1. I have been 2. you have been 3. he has been	1. we have been 2. you have been 3. they have been
Past Perfect Tense		1. I had been 2. you had been 3. he had been	1. we had been 2. you had been 3. they had been
Future Perfect Tense		1. I shall have been 2. you will have been 3. he will have been	1. we shall have been 2. you will have been 3. they will have been

SUBJUNCTIVE MOOD

		Singular	Plural
Present Tense		1. I be 2. you be 3. he be	1. we be 2. you be 3. they be
Past Tense		1. I were 2. you were 3. he were	1. we were 2. you were 3. they were
Present Perfect Tense		1. I have been 2. you have been 3. he have been	1. we have been 2. you have been 3. they have been
Past Perfect Tense		1. I had been 2. you had been 3. he had been	1. we had been 2. you had been 3. they had been

IMPERATIVE MOOD
Present Tense   be   be

	Present	Past	Perfect
INFINITIVES	to be		to have been
PARTICIPLES	being	been	having been
GERUNDS	being		having been

207 CONJUGATION OF THE VERB *SEE*
Active Voice

INDICATIVE MOOD		Singular	Plural
Present Tense		1. I see	1. we see
		2. you see	2. you see
		3. he sees	3. they see
Past Tense		1. I saw	1. we saw
		2. you saw	2. you saw
		3. he saw	3. they saw
Future Tense		1. I shall see	1. we shall see
		2. you will see	2. you will see
		3. he will see	3. they will see
Present Perfect Tense		1. I have seen	1. we have seen
		2. you have seen	2. you have seen
		3. he has seen	3. they have seen
Past Perfect Tense		1. I had seen	1. we had seen
		2. you had seen	2. you had seen
		3. he had seen	3. they had seen
Future Perfect Tense		1. I shall have seen	1. we shall have seen
		2. you will have seen	2. you will have seen
		3. he will have seen	3. they will have seen

SUBJUNCTIVE MOOD		Singular	Plural
Present Tense		1. I see	1. we see
		2. you see	2. you see
		3. he see	3. they see
Past Tense		1. I saw	1. we saw
		2. you saw	2. you saw
		3. he saw	3. they saw
Present Perfect Tense		1. I have seen	1. we have seen
		2. you have seen	2. you have seen
		3. he have seen	3. they have seen
Past Perfect Tense		1. I had seen	1. we had seen
		2. you had seen	2. you had seen
		3. he had seen	3. they had seen

IMPERATIVE MOOD

	see		see

	Present	*Past*	*Perfect*
Present Tense			
INFINITIVES	to see		to have seen
PARTICIPLES	seeing	seen	having seen
GERUNDS	seeing		having seen

208 CONJUGATION OF THE VERB *SEE*

Passive Voice

INDICATIVE MOOD	*Singular*	*Plural*
Present Tense	1. I am seen 2. you are seen 3. he is seen	1. we are seen 2. you are seen 3. they are seen
Past Tense	1. I was seen 2. you were seen 3. he was seen	1. we were seen 2. you were seen 3. they were seen
Future Tense	1. I shall be seen 2. you will be seen 3. he will be seen	1. we shall be seen 2. you will be seen 3. they will be seen
Present Perfect Tense	1. I have been seen 2. you have been seen 3. he has been seen	1. we have been seen 2. you have been seen 3. they have been seen
Past Perfect Tense	1. I had been seen 2. you had been seen 3. he had been seen	1. we had been seen 2. you had been seen 3. they had been seen
Future Perfect Tense	1. I shall have been seen 2. you will have been seen 3. he will have been seen	1. we shall have been seen 2. you will have been seen 3. they will have been seen

SUBJUNCTIVE MOOD		
Present Tense	1. I be seen 2. you be seen 3. he be seen	1. we be seen 2. you be seen 3. they be seen
Past Tense	1. I were seen 2. you were seen 3. he were seen	1. we were seen 2. you were seen 3. they were seen
Present Perfect Tense	1. I have been seen 2. you have been seen 3. he have been seen	1. we have been seen 2. you have been seen 3. they have been seen
Past Perfect Tense	1. I had been seen 2. you had been seen 3. he had been seen	1. we had been seen 2. you had been seen 3. they had been seen

IMPERATIVE MOOD		
Present Tense	be seen	be seen

	Present	Past	Perfect
INFINITIVES	to be seen		to have been seen
PARTICIPLES	being seen	seen	having been seen
GERUNDS	being seen		having been seen

209 CONJUGATION OF THE VERB *SEE* — PROGRESSIVE FORM

Active Voice

INDICATIVE MOOD		*Singular*	*Plural*
Present Tense	1.	I am seeing	1. we are seeing
	2.	you are seeing	2. you are seeing
	3.	he is seeing	3. they are seeing
Past Tense	1.	I was seeing	1. we were seeing
	2.	you were seeing	2. you were seeing
	3.	he was seeing	3. they were seeing
Future Tense	1.	I shall be seeing	1. we shall be seeing
	2.	you will be seeing	2. you will be seeing
	3.	he will be seeing	3. they will be seeing
Present Perfect Tense	1.	I have been seeing	1. we have been seeing
	2.	you have been see-ing	2. you have been see-ing
	3.	he has been seeing	3. they have been see-ing
Past Perfect Tense	1.	I had been seeing	1. we had been seeing
	2.	you had been seeing	2. you had been seeing
	3.	he had been seeing	3. they had been see-ing
Future Perfect Tense	1.	I shall have been seeing	1. we shall have been seeing
	2.	you will have been seeing	2. you will have been seeing
	3.	he will have been seeing	3. they will have been seeing

SUBJUNCTIVE MOOD			
Present Tense	1.	I be seeing	1. we be seeing
	2.	you be seeing	2. you be seeing
	3.	he be seeing	3. they be seeing
Past Tense	1.	I were seeing	1. we were seeing
	2.	you were seeing	2. you were seeing
	3.	he were seeing	3. they were seeing

	Present	Perfect
INFINITIVES	to be seeing	to have been seeing
PARTICIPLES		having been seeing

210 CONJUGATION OF THE VERB *SEE* — PROGRESSIVE FORM

Passive Voice

INDICATIVE MOOD	*Singular*	*Plural*
	1. I am being seen	1. we are being seen
Present Tense	2. you are being seen	2. you are being seen
	3. he is being seen	3. they are being seen
	1. I was being seen	1. we were being seen
Past Tense	2. you were being seen	2. you were being seen
	3. he was being seen	3. they were being seen

211 Besides the tense forms given in 206, 207, 208, two other forms are frequently used: the **progressive** (209, 210) and the **emphatic.**

212 The **progressive form** represents action as continuing at the time noted. This form is also called the **present (past, future,** etc.) **continuous** by many grammarians. It is made by placing some form of the verb *to be* before the present participle (201):

I *am seeing*—you *are seeing*—he *is seeing.*

Although the present-participle form is used in making the progressive verb phrase, the participle is here considered not as a participle but as a part of the entire verb phrase:

David *is painting* a picture. (*Painting*, though present participle in form, is here considered to be a part of the verb phrase *is painting*.)

213 The **emphatic form** gives emphasis to the present or past form of the verb in the active voice (184) by the use of *do, does,* or *did*. Forms of *do* are used also in negative statements and in questions without emphasis:

I *do see.*   She *does see.*   He *did see.* (emphatic)
Do you see?   I *do* not see. (not emphatic)

214 The **synopsis** of a verb is the correct arrangement of its moods (187–189); voices (184–185), and tenses (191–196) in **one person** (69) and **number** (73); it is an abbreviated conjugation (205).

215 SYNOPSIS OF THE VERB *SEE*

in the Third Person, Singular Number

INDICATIVE MOOD	*Active*	*Passive*
Present Tense	he sees	he is seen
Past Tense	he saw	he was seen
Future Tense	he will see	he will be seen
Present Perfect Tense	he has seen	he has been seen
Past Perfect Tense	he had seen	he had been seen
Future Perfect Tense	he will have seen	he will have been seen

SUBJUNCTIVE MOOD

Present Tense	he see	he be seen
Past Tense	he saw	he were seen
Present Perfect Tense	he have seen	he have been seen
Past Perfect Tense	he had seen	he had been seen

(The imperative mood is used in the second person only.)

Usage

216 Five frequently used verbs that cause much trouble are the following: *come, go, do, see, give.*

> Bob *came* (not *come*) yesterday.
> He had *come* (not *came*) when I left.
> She had *gone* (not *went*) when you came.
> May *did* (not *done*) the work well.
> She has *done* (not *did*) good work.
> I *saw* (not *seen*) her yesterday.
> Tom had *seen* (not *saw*) the show.
> Ann *gave* (not *give*) me this book.
> Pat had *given* (not *gave*) her a camera.

217 These three pairs of verbs are often confused: *lie—lay, sit—set, rise—raise.*

Lie, sit, and *rise* are always intransitive (175) in their usual meanings. *Lay, set,* and *raise* are usually transitive (174) and, therefore, must have an object to complete the meaning:

> Let us *lie* here and rest.   I *laid* the book there yesterday.
> She *sits* by the window to read.   I *set* the box on the shelf.
> The cake did not *rise* well.   Did you *raise* the flag?

♦ The verbs *lay* and *set* may be used as intransitives in certain of their secondary meanings:

> The hen *lays* well.
> The sun *set* at six o'clock yesterday.
> This jelly did not *set* well.
> We eagerly *set* out on our long journey.

218 *May* is used to express permission; *can* refers to ability:

> *May* I go to town?   *Can* the bird fly?

Some writers use *can* for permission, but this usage is more often than not disapproved for written use as being colloquial or informal.

219 Use *shall* in the first person and *will* in the second and third persons for the simple future tense:

> I *shall* sing this afternoon.
> You *will* succeed.   He *will* stay at home.

220 To express determination, desire, or a promise, reverse the normal order and use *will* in the first person and *shall* in the second and third persons:

> I *will* be there.
> You *shall* not go.   They *shall* be brought to justice.

221 In asking questions in the first person, use *shall*; in the second or third person, use the form that would be correct in the answer:

> *Shall* you leave tomorrow? (The answer is "I *shall*.")
> *Will* John defy me? (He *will*.)

222 Use *shall* in all persons in object (noun) clauses after verbs of *deciding, wishing, demanding, willing*, etc.:

> He insists that they *shall* not follow him.

223 In an indirect quotation (expressing the thought but not the actual words of the speaker) use the tense form correct for the speaker:

> John says that he *shall* win. (He said, "I *shall* win.")

224 The uses of *should* and *would* correspond to those of *shall* and *will*:

1. For simple future, use *should* with the first person, and use *would* with the second and third.

2. For determination, reverse the order.

3. In questions in the first person, use *should*. (See 221) In questions in the second and third persons, use the form which would be correct in the answer.

4. In indirect discourse (indirect quotation), use the form that would be correct if the quotation were direct.

◆The rules governing the use of *shall* and *will*, *should* and *would*, are seldom stressed because of a wide variation in actual practice that makes them interchangeable.

225 *Had ought to* is never correct as a combination for *ought to* or *should*:

> He *should* (or *ought to*, not *had ought to*) work.

226 The use of the word *loan* as a verb is interchangeable with *lend* in matters of money but is more restricted in other meanings:

> He *loaned* me ten dollars.   He *lent* his bicycle.

227 Do not confuse *leave* and *let*, *learn* and *teach*. To *leave* means *to go away from*; *to let* means *to permit* or *to allow*:

She will *let* (not *leave*) us use her pen.

To learn means *to get information; to teach* means *to give information*:

He will *teach* (not *learn*) me to paint.

228 *Accept* and *except* are often confused. *To accept* means *to take; to except* means *to leave out* or *to exclude*:

I *accept* the gift.

If we *except* her picture from the show, she will feel hurt.

229 Although *ain't* is usually condemned as nonstandard, we need some good word to take its place (662):

The roses *aren't* (not *ain't*) in bloom yet.

I am to blame, *am I not* (not *ain't*)?

In England, the form *aren't I* is considered correct in the preceding sentence. Although this form has gained favor in this country, some American authorities still classify it as informal.

230 Never use *of* as a substitute for *have*:

She should *have* (not *of*) gone home.

231 Some authorities object to the formal written use of *and* for *to* with *try*:

Questionable: Try *and* help him.

Correct: Try *to* help him.

However, *and* is never used with *tries, tried,* or *trying*.

232 After certain words the *to* is generally omitted from the infinitive (199). Some of these words are *bid, dare, let, make, help, need, see*:

Let us (without *to*) go to the show.

233 There is some objection to the use of *but what* for *but that* after negative forms of verbs:

Questionable: He did not know *but what* I left.

Informal: He did not know *but that* I left.

Formal: He did not know *that* I left.

234 Do not use *help but* in the sense of *avoid* in formal writing:

Colloquial: He could not *help but* laugh.

Formal: He could not *help* laughing.

235 The **split infinitive**—the use of a word between the parts of an infinitive (199)—is not at all incorrect, but it usually makes an awkward sentence unless carefully controlled:

Awkward: She told me *to not help* him.
Better: She told me *not to help* him.

Agreement of Verb and Subject

236 Words that are joined to a subject by *with, accompanied by, together with, as well as, no less than,* or *including* do not change the number of the subject:

The teacher, as well as the students, *was* there.
The students, as well as the teacher, *were* there.

237 Two or more singular subjects joined by *or* or *nor* require a singular verb:

Neither Esther nor Ruth *was* present.

238 When a subject is composed of both singular and plural forms joined by *or* or *nor*, the verb must agree with the nearer subject:

Two other boys or Henry *is* to blame!   Neither he nor the boys *play* golf.

239 In a sentence beginning with *here* or *there*, the number of the verb is determined by the number of the substantive following it:

There *is* a book on the table.   There *are* hats in the window.
Here *are* Bob and Sue.   There go Joe and Fred.

♦ When *there* is used as an introductory word, as in the first two sentences, it is called an **expletive**. An expletive is a word which, without special meaning of its own, introduces a subject or object that follows. *It* is another word frequently used in this way:

It is good to be here.   Make *it* clear that she is invited.

240 A collective noun (59) takes a singular verb when the group is considered as a unit and takes a plural verb when the individuals are considered (92):

Our football team *is* popular.   The team *have* received their sweaters.

241 In expressions such as *one of the girls who, one of the trees which,* and *one of the persons that,* the verb in the relative clause agrees with the antecedent of the relative pronoun (135):

He is one of those teachers who *are* inspiring. (The antecedent of *who* is *teachers*.)
She is the only one of the group that *understands*. (The antecedent of *that* is *one*.)

242 *Each, either, neither, someone, somebody, anyone, anybody, everyone, everybody, no one, nobody, one,* and *a person* are singular (163, 164):

> Each of the students *was* (not *were*) questioned.
>
> Neither Rosa nor Tim *was* (not *were*) home.

243 If *plenty, abundance,* or *rest* is modified by a phrase introduced by *of,* the verb agrees with the noun in the phrase:

> Plenty of potatoes *are* grown in Colorado.
>
> An *abundance* of meat *was* provided.

♦ Fractions are used in this same way:

> One third of the paper *was* sold.   One fifth of the boats *were* lost.

244 If the word *number* is preceded by *a* and followed by *of,* it takes a plural verb; if it is preceded by *the,* it requires a singular verb:

> A number of men *were* hurt.   The number of accidents *is* great.

245 A noun that refers to an amount of money, a space of time, or a unit of measurement is singular in meaning even though the form is plural:

> Fifty cents *is* the price.   Ten miles *is* a long way to walk.

246 A phrase (389) between the subject (except in the case of a following relative clause as in 241) and the verb does not affect the verb:

> One of the girls *is* my friend.

247 If the subject of the verb is made up of two or more words joined by *and,* the verb is plural. (If the two are thought of as a unit, the verb is singular: Bread and butter *is* a good food.) In asking questions beginning with verbs, it is necessary to be careful:

> Helen and Grace *are* here.   *Are* Grace and her sister here?

248 If a subject consists of two or more nouns, only one of which is expressed, the verb is plural:

> A red and a blue book *are* on the desk.

249 A verb introduced by a relative pronoun (135) has the same number and person as the noun or pronoun to which it refers:

> He gave the book to me who *am* (not *is*) its owner.

Sequence of Tenses

250 If the verb in the main clause (397) is in the past tense (193), the verb in the dependent clause (398) may be in the past tense:

> Jennifer said that she *expected* to go home.

251 The past tense in the main clause (397) may be followed by the present tense in the dependent clause (398) when it expresses a general truth:

Columbus believed that the earth *is* round.

252 An idea once established as truth, now known to be untrue, is expressed in the past tense:

The ancients believed that the earth *was* flat.

253 SEQUENCE OF TENSES IN INDIRECT DISCOURSE (Reported Speech)

    (a) Present or "now" time, or possible future time
    (b) Intended or completed action in past time
    (c) Intended or completed action in future time

1. **Present**
Ben *says* that (a) he *is going* (*goes*) with us.
    (b) he *was going* (*went*) with us.
    (c) he *will be going* (*will go*) with us.

2. **Past**
Ben *said* that (a) he *is going* (*goes*) with us.
    (b) he *was going* (*went*) with us.
    (c) he *will be going* (*will go*) with us.

3. **Future**
Ben *will say* that (a) he *is going* (*goes*) with us.
    (b) he *was going* (*went*) with us.
    (c) he *will be going* (*will go*) with us.

4. **Present Perfect**
Ben *has said* that (a) he *is going* (*goes*) with us.
    (b) he *was going* (*went*) with us.
    (c) he *would be going* (*would go*) with us.

5. **Past Perfect**
Ben *had said* that (a) he *is going* (*goes*) with us.
    (b) he *was going* (*went*) with us.
    (b) he *had been going* (*had gone*) with us.
    (c) he *would have been going* (*would have gone*) with us.

6. *Future Perfect*
Ben *will have said* that (a) he *is going* (*goes*) with us.
    (b) he *was going* (*went*) with us.
    (b) he *had been going* (*had gone*) with us.
    (c) he *would have been going* (*would have gone*) with us.

This chart shows all the possible relationships. Numbers 1, 2, 4, and 5 are used in statement-of-fact situations; numbers 3 and 6 reflect a qualifying or conditional statement which suggests that a clause, such as "if he were asked," has not been expressed though it is implied.

Special Uses of Voice, Tense, and Number

254 Do not shift illogically from the active voice (184) to the passive (185) in the same sentence.

As we came over the hill, we *saw a deer* (not a *deer was seen*).

255 Use the active voice (184) unless there is some self-evident reason for using the passive:

We *heard a noise* (not A *noise was heard*).

256 In expressing a **wish or a condition contrary to fact**, use *were*, not *was*:

If I *were* he, I'd go home.   I wish she *were* the governor.

257 In a past **condition not contrary to fact**, the indicative mood (187) is used, not the subjunctive (189) as in 256:

If John *was* present, I did not see him.

258 After *as if* and *as though*, use the subjunctive *were*:

She speaks as though she *were* angry.

259 With words expressing **command** or **necessity**, use either the present subjunctive form (189) or a verb-phrase:

It is necessary that the boy *be* (or *should be*) dismissed immediately.
It was necessary that he *be* dismissed.

260 Use *are* or *were* with *you*, even when the pronoun is singular:

Edgar, you *were* there.   *Are* you there, now?

261 When one subject is affirmative and the other negative, the verb agrees with the affirmative:

Your honesty, not your pleas, *causes* me to relent.

262 In the use of **arithmetical expressions** there has been disagreement as to the correct verb forms, but the following are accepted:

Six divided by three *is* two.   Seven minus two *is* five.
One fourth of twelve *is* three.   Five plus three *is* eight.
Five times two *are* ten.   Three and four *are* seven.

263 When the **infinitive** (199) refers to a time coincident with that of the main verb or some time after it, use the present infinitive:

I intended *to sing* (not *to have sung*).

The **present infinitive** (199, 206) may be used with a main verb in any tense, as follows:

She wishes *to meet* you.   She had wished *to meet* you.
She wished *to meet* you.   She will wish *to meet* you.
She has wished *to meet* you.   She will have wished *to meet* you.

When the **perfect infinitive** (199, 206) is used with a verb in the past tense or in the past perfect tense (193, 194) expressing *desire, hope,* or *duty,* it indicates that something interfered with the desire, hope, or duty:

She wished *to have seen* you. (She did not see you.)

I hoped *to have met* you. (I did not meet you.)

When the present infinitive is used after one of these verbs there is an element of uncertainty:

He hoped *to meet* you. (Whether he did or not is uncertain.)

The use of the perfect infinitive (199, 206) after such verbs as *seem, appear,* and *know* shows that the event denoted by the infinitive took place before the time indicated by the verb:

Bob seems *to have succeeded.*

264 It is incorrect to use a present participle when indicating an action previous to that expressed by the main verb:

He has been away three days, *having left* (not *leaving*) last Monday.

Uses of the Verbals

265 The **infinitive** (199, 232) has many uses:

1. The infinitive used as a **noun** (56, 61-5):
   a. **Subject of a verb** (95): *To win* is not easy.
   b. **Predicate nominative** (96): What she wants is *to win.*
   c. **Object of a verb** (102): He likes *to write.*
   d. **Nominative case in apposition with the subject** (100): His aim, *to succeed,* is commendable.
   e. **Objective case in apposition with object** (111): She has one great desire, *to succeed.*

◆ An infinitive may be used much as any other noun (393).

2. The infinitive used as an **adjective** (277): The house *to be sold* is new.
3. The infinitive used as an **adverb** (316): Mary came *to see* us.

DIAGRAM—An infinitive used as subject:

To succeed is his intention.

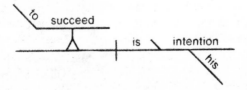

266 The gerund (56, 61-4, 200) has many noun uses, as follows:

1. Subject of a verb: *Stealing* is wrong.
2. Object of verb: I heard the *roaring* of the river.
3. Object of preposition: Were they punished for *cheating?*
4. Apposition: His work, *mining*, was dangerous.
5. Predicate nominative: Her work is *painting* signs.

Diagram—A gerund used as **subject** (266-1) and having an object:
Running races is good exercise.

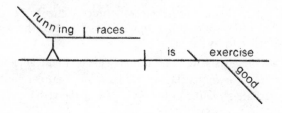

Diagram—A gerund used as **object** (266-2) and having an object:
The boys dislike *picking* cotton.

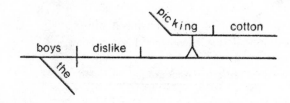

267 Most authorities agree that a verbal may be considered a pure noun when it has lost the verbal idea; when it may be pluralized; when it may be preceded by an article and followed by a preposition; or when it is the name of an art, a course of study, or some form of activity:

We attended the *wedding.*   The *rowing* of the boat was easy.
I know Bob's *drawings.*   I am taking a course in *writing.*

268 A compound gerund is formed by placing a noun before a gerund: *mountain climbing, skin diving*

The gerund is also called **verbal noun** or **participial noun** (200).
♦ There are some grammarians who believe there is a difference between the gerund and the verbal noun, but the difference is one of identification rather than of use and function.

269 The **participle** is a verbal (198, 201) which is used as an adjective. It has the same uses as the regular adjective (275):

    1. **Attributive** (276):

        The *running* stream is beauti-   A *broken* limb of the tree has
        ful.   fallen.

    2. **Predicate adjective** (179-4, 278, 289):

        The game was *thrilling*.   The boy is *discouraged*.

    3. **Appositive adjective** (277):

        The girl, *running* swiftly, soon disappeared.

        The limb, *broken* by the wind, has fallen down.

    The participle ending in *ing* sometimes seems to be a pure adjective, and at other times it is thought of as a part of the verb-phrase in the progressive form (212):

    The *gleaming* stars are beautiful. (resembles a pure **adjective**)

    The stars, *gleaming* in the sky, are beautiful. (**regular participle**)

    The stars are *gleaming* in the sky. (**part of the verb**)

    The past participle (201) is sometimes used as an adjective and sometimes as the main part of the verb in the passive voice (185):

    This drama, *written* by Thornton Wilder, is my favorite. (**adjective**)

    This book *was written* by Rachel Carson. (**part of the passive verb form**)

DIAGRAM—A participle (201) having an object:

    John, *fearing defeat*, encouraged his comrades.

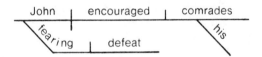

270 A noun or pronoun introducing a gerund is usually in the possessive case (116, 127):

    He approved *Ann's* (not *Ann*) selling the book.

    He did not like *my* (not *me*) going away.

    This rule is not rigidly observed in conversation and informal writing.

   ◆ It will sometimes require close observation to distinguish the participle from the gerund:

    We referred to the girl *playing* tennis. (**participle**)

    We referred to the girl's *playing* tennis. (**gerund**)

271 A **participial phrase** (390-3) or a **prepositional gerund phrase** should have a substantive (47) that it can logically modify expressed in the sentence. When the substantive is omitted, the modifying phrase is said to be **dangling**. Dangling modifiers often result in absurdities. Be sure to give modifiers something to modify (451):

> *Running to the window,* I saw a fire (not a *fire was seen*). (390-3) (The participial phrase *running to the window* modifies *I*. The fire was not running to the window.)
>
> *By working hard,* we finished the task (not the *task was finished*). (390-4) (The prepositional phrase *by working hard,* which has a gerund as the object of the preposition, modifies *we*.)
>
> *Sitting in the moonlight,* we enjoyed the music (not the *music was enjoyed*).

♦ A few set phrases, such as *generally speaking, considering everything,* are understood to modify the entire sentence, not any particular substantive in it; they are then called **sentence modifiers**.

Punctuation of participles and gerunds is very important. Note the use of the comma (499) in the examples just given. If a participial phrase begins the sentence, it is followed by a comma:

> *Running quickly,* the girl won the race.

The absolute construction (99) is set off from the rest of the sentence by a comma or commas:

> *The game being ended,* we went home.

Sometimes the word *being* is omitted from the absolute construction, but the comma is used:

> *The matter* (being) *adjusted,* we felt relieved.

Nonrestrictive phrases (phrases not necessary to the meaning of the rest of the sentence) are set off by commas (499):

> The man *sitting by the desk* is the principal. (**necessary**—no commas used)
>
> The old man, *sitting idly in the sun,* dreamed of other days. (**unnecessary**—commas used)

272 The **subject of an infinitive** (108, 199) is in the objective case:

> We asked *him* to go. (*Him* is the subject of *to go*.)
>
> Jack asked *her* to sing. (*Her* is the subject of *to sing*.)

273 In an **infinitive clause** (401) a predicate noun (96) or a predicate pronoun (145-2) used after *to be* is in the objective case to agree with the subject of the infinitive (109):

> You thought us to be *them*.
>
> They took me to be *her*.

274 If the infinitive *to be* has no subject, the predicate noun or the predicate pronoun following it is in the nominative case (109):

He was thought to be *I*.

I was believed to be *she*.

Adjectives

275 An **adjective** is a modifier (7) which describes or limits a substantive (47). It may be a word or a group of words (7, 8, 9, 42):

We saw *beautiful* flowers.

Those flowers *on the desk* are roses. (*Those* is a simple modifier; the group is a phrase modifier, 390-1.)

Those boys *whom you saw* are students. (*Those* is a simple modifier; the group is a clause modifier, 408.)

The adjective is used effectively in painting word pictures—describing (553). Note the effect of the added modifiers (7) in the illustrations below:

Near the house stood a tree. (**unimpressive**)

Above the gray, old-fashioned, stone dwelling a tall, slender eucalyptus tree waved its feathery branches in the summer morning sunlight. (**vivid**)

Adjectives are used in three ways: **attributive, appositive,** and **predicate.**

276 The **attributive** use of the adjective is that of the direct modifier that precedes the substantive:

The man wore a *dark* suit.

◆ Adjectives in a series are separated by commas (505):

A *beautiful, tall, slender* pine stood nearby.

277 The **appositive** use of the adjective directly follows the substantive that it modifies:

The speaker, *tall* and *graceful*, soon won the audience. (The adjectives *tall* and *graceful* explain the appearance of the speaker. The adjective used appositively is set off by a comma or commas.)

278 The **predicate** use of the adjective (179-4, 289) is to complete the meaning of the predicate and modify the subject:

The work was *difficult*.   Mountains are *beautiful*.

The predicate adjective is usually joined to the subject by a linking verb (180). (But also see 289.)

279 An adjective that describes a substantive (47) by expressing some quality belonging to it is called a **descriptive adjective:**

We saw *tall* trees.   They climbed *high* hills.

280 An adjective that describes a substantive or that limits its meaning without expressing a quality is called a **limiting** or **definitive adjective:**

    She sent us *those* books.   We saw *many* trees.

281 The limiting or definitive adjectives include **pronouns used as adjectives** (pronominal adjectives, both indefinite and demonstrative, 138, 139, 140), **numeral adjectives,** and **the articles.**

    Pronouns in the possessive case (116, 117) are sometimes called **possessive adjectives** (131, 146):

    John lost *his* book.

    ♦ The possessive adjective is also pronominal, 140.

The **pronominal adjectives** (140) are given under the treatment of pronouns (131, 138, 139), but further illustrations of their uses are given here. Be sure to distinguish between the pronoun use and the adjective use:

    This book is a grammar. (**adjective**)
    This is a book. (**pronoun,** 138)
    Each should bring a book. (**pronoun**)
    Each student should bring a book. (**adjective**)
    We saw *her* at the movies. (**pronoun in the objective case**)
    We saw *her* book on the desk. (**pronoun in the possessive case:** also called a **possessive adjective,** 131)

282 **Numeral adjectives** indicate number. There are two classes which are generally used: **cardinal** and **ordinal.**

283 The **cardinal** number indicates how many items there are in a group or set:

    We saw *three* ships.

284 The **ordinal** number gives the order of the items in a sequence:

    He won the *third* prize.

285 The adjectives *a, an,* and *the* are called **articles.**

286 *A* and *an* are called **indefinite articles** because they do not point out particular persons, places, or things—*a* and *an* are modified forms of *one:*

    The camper saw *a* deer and *an* eagle. (*An* is used before a word beginning with one of the vowel sounds—*a, e, i, o, u.* Before a consonant sound, *a* is used.)

287 *The* is called the **definite article** because it points out a particular member of a class of persons, places, or things—*the* is a modified form of *that.*

    This is *the* book we need.

♦ *The* may also be used to indicate a generalized noun as a representative of its class:

We have now studied *the* noun, *the* verb, and *the* adjective.

288 The **proper adjective** is derived from a proper noun (55) or is a proper noun used as an adjective and is written with a capital letter.

Although he is a *Chinese* student, he enjoys the *Colorado* climate.

289 A **predicate adjective** (278) completes the verb and relates to the subject:

She looks *cheerful.*

Predicate adjectives are used with the linking verbs, such as *be* and *become* and such verbs of the senses as: *seems, appears, looks, tastes, feels, smells, sounds;* also *proves, remains, turns, grows, stays, continues.* Avoid substituting an adverb (316) for an adjective after a linking verb (180):

The rose smells *sweet* (not *sweetly*).

He looks *bad* (not *badly*) since his illness.

♦ Predicate adjectives (and predicate nominatives, 96) may also occur after certain verbs (104) in the passive (185):

She was considered *intelligent.*

290 Many words commonly used as **pronouns** may be used as modifying **adjectives** (138, 139, 281):

That hat is made of fur.   I know *what* man you mean.

Which horse is yours?   *Any* boy can do *that* work.

♦ When the noun which is modified is omitted, each of the adjectives of this class becomes a pronoun (138, 139, 281):

That is made of fur. (**pronoun**)

Comparison of Adjectives

291 Adjectives have **three degrees of comparison: positive, comparative,** and **superlative.**

292 The **positive degree** expresses a quality without comparison:

Joe is *tall.*

293 The **comparative degree** expresses a higher or lower degree than the positive when two persons or things are compared:

Kay is *taller* than Joan.   Joan is *less talkative* than Kay.

294 The **superlative degree** is the highest or lowest degree when more than two persons or things are compared:

Bob is the *tallest* boy in the club.   He is also the *least talkative* member.

295 Comparison is indicated in three ways:

1. By adding *er* or *est* to the positive degree: *large—larger—largest.*
2. By prefixing *more* and *most* or *less* and *least: graceful—more graceful—most graceful; practical—less practical—least practical.*
3. By irregular inflection: *bad—worse—worst.*

Forms of Comparison

Positive	Comparative	Superlative
long	longer	longest
beautiful	more beautiful	most beautiful
beautiful	less beautiful	least beautiful
much	more	most

296 Use the comparative degree (293), not the superlative, in comparing two objects:

He is the *older* of the two boys.   She is the *more gifted* of the two.
♦ The familiar expression, "Put your *best* foot forward," is correct as an idiomatic construction.

297 Certain adjectives that express **absolute qualities** do not logically, and in the strictest sense, admit of comparison; but many good writers do compare them regularly while others use *more nearly* and *most nearly* as an alternative use. The words *unique, perfect, square, straight, endless, dead, perpendicular* are in this group:

This is the *most* perfect rose. (questionable as **redundant**)
This is the *most nearly* perfect rose. (preferred as **logically acceptable**)

However, when such words are not used with their basic literal meaning, they may be compared:

This is the *deadest* party I ever attended.

298 The comparative is used with *than* because only two things (whether individuals or groups) are involved:

The new machine runs *faster* than the old one. (Two groups are compared.)

When comparing something with the rest of the class of things to which it belongs, use *other, else,* or some such word:

John works faster than any *other* boy in school. (John is compared with the rest of the boys.)

Usage

299 When a numeral adjective and a noun form a compound adjective, the singular form of the noun is used:

a thirty-*day* vacation, a five-*foot* fence.

300 When a plural adjective modifies a noun, as a rule the noun becomes plural:

He rode ten *miles* (not *mile*).

301 Words such as *dozen, head, score, gross,* and *hundred* retain their singular form when preceded by an adjective expressing number:

He kept three *head* of horses in his stable.

302 *This* and *that* are the only adjectives inflected for number. *This* and *that* modify singular nouns: *these* and *those,* plural nouns:

I like *this* kind of book and *these* kinds of pencils.

She prefers *those* kinds of roses and *that* kind of aster

303 *First* and *last,* when used with adjectives that express number, are placed before the adjectives to make the meaning specific:

Omit the *last* ten pages.

304 When two or more adjectives modify the same noun, clearness requires that an article (*a, an,* or *the*) be used before the first adjective only:

a blue, gray, and white bird. (one bird)

305 When two or more adjectives modify different nouns, one expressed and the others understood (248), an article is used before each adjective:

The large and *the* small house are mine. (two houses)

306 *Less* indicates amount; *fewer* denotes number:

We hope for *less* rain this month.

Fewer than twenty girls played ball.

307 The article *a* or *an* is not used after *kind of* or *sort of:*

What *kind of* (not *kind of a*) book is that?

308 When two or more nouns are used to refer to the same person or thing, an article should be used before the first noun only:

The teacher and mayor (one person) of the town was loved by everyone.

309 When nouns used together refer to different persons or things, an article should be used before each noun:

The teacher and *the* minister are popular. (two persons)

310 In comparison use *so* instead of *as* after a negative such as *not:*

She is not *so* tall as Jane. (*So* is used in the negative statement.)

She is *as* tall as Mary. (*As* is used in the positive statement.)

311 Do not use an adjective as an adverb. Do not use *sure* for *surely*, *real* for *really*, *some* for *somewhat*, *different* for *differently*:

>She *surely* (not *sure*) is busy.

>He was *really* (not *real*) pleased to help.

♦ Some adverbs have two forms, one with *ly* and one like the adjective. The short form may be used in some sentences:

>Drive *slow*.   He went *slowly* down the street.

312 Remember that verbs of the senses, such as *smell, taste, feel, look,* are generally completed by adjectives, not by adverbs:

>He looks *tired*. (**adjective**, 179-4, 278, 289)

313 After any words used as linking verbs (180), the adjective (278, 289) form, not the adverb, should be used: *seem, become, appear, prove, remain, keep, stay, continue.*

314 The verbs *turn* and *grow* used in the sense of *become* are followed by an adjective:

>The leaves turn *red*.   The clouds grow *dark*.

315 The suffix *-like* may be added to many nouns to form an adjective: *homelike, lifelike, swanlike.*

However, *-like* should not be added indiscriminately to those adjectives for which a word with this meaning already exists.

Incorrect: The flame was *bluelike*.

Correct: The flame was *bluish*.

Adverbs

316 An adverb may modify a **verb** (170–180), an **adjective** (275–280), another **adverb**, a **verbal** (198–201), a **preposition** (341–346), a **conjunction** (365–369), or occasionally a **substantive** (47, 61):

>She sings *beautifully*. (*Beautifully* modifies the verb *sings*.)

>He is a *very* great orator. (*Very* modifies the adjective *great*.)

>She smiled *rather* sadly. (*Rather* modifies the adverb *sadly*.)

>By working *faithfully*, she won success. (*Faithfully* modfies the gerund *working*.)

>The little boy, smiling *happily*, ran to meet his father. (*Happily* modifies the participle *smiling*.)

>She has learned to write *clearly*. (*Clearly* modifies the infinitive *to write*.)

>He was *almost* under the tree. (*Almost* modifies the preposition *under*.)

>She came *just* before I left. (*Just* modifies the conjunction *before*.)

>*Nearly* all of them were lost. (*Nearly* modifies the indefinite pronoun *all*, see 139.)

The *newly* rich were not invited. (*Newly* modifies the noun equivalent *rich*; see 61. Compare 714.)

♦ Not all grammarians agree and some state that an adverb may not modify the preposition alone, but modifies the entire phrase introduced by the preposition. They also say that an adverb may not modify a conjunction, but modifies the clause introduced by it. Therefore in the sentences above it could be said that *almost* modifies the phrase *under the tree*, and that *just* modifies the clause *before I left*. Sometimes an adverb appears to modify an entire sentence and is therefore called a **sentence adverb:**

Evidently, he doesn't care what we think.

The adverb may be a single word, a phrase (8), or a clause (9):

The child sang *joyfully*. (**word**)

The child sang *with joy*. (**phrase**)

The child sang *because he was happy*. (**clause**)

The addition of adverb modifiers gives life to expression, as is shown by the illustration below (see also 275):

The president spoke.

The new president spoke *briefly* but *enthusiastically* about the plans for the coming year.

Such expressions as *one by one, by and by, now and then*, and *little by little* are called **phrasal adverbs.**

317   According to their use in a sentence, adverbs may be grouped into three classes: **simple, interrogative,** and **conjunctive.**

318   A **simple adverb** is a simple modifier:

She spoke *kindly*.

319   An **interrogative adverb** is used in asking a question:

Where have you been?

320   A **conjunctive adverb** is used to connect independent clauses (367, 397). Some common conjunctive adverbs are: *accordingly, also, anyhow, besides, consequently, however, moreover, nevertheless, otherwise, still, then, therefore, yet:*

Joe did not like the course; *nevertheless*, he worked hard and made a good grade.

Joe did not like the course; he worked hard, *nevertheless*, and made a good grade.

A semicolon (490) is used between clauses joined by a conjunctive adverb whether the adverb begins the second clause, as in the first sentence above, or is used within it, as in the second sentence.

321   **Simple adverbs** are divided into classes: adverbs of **manner, time, place, degree,** and **number.**

322 Adverbs of **manner** indicate how the action takes place:
He walked *proudly.*

323 Adverbs of **time** indicate when the action takes place:
Fred left *yesterday.*

324 Adverbs of **place** indicate where the action takes place:
Some of my friends were *there.*

325 Adverbs of **degree** indicate how much or to what extent:
She seemed *rather* confident.

326 Adverbs of **number** indicate order or how many times:
He arrived *first.*   He came only *once.*

327 Adverbs, like adjectives, have **three degrees** of comparison (291–295) —positive, comparative, and superlative: *slowly—more slowly— most slowly.* In general, this is possible only for adverbs of manner.

Usage

328 Do not use the adjective *most* for the adverb *almost* (671):
It seems that *almost* (not *most*) all the students are here. (See 316 and 325)

329 *Good* is an adjective; *well* is usually an adverb. Do not confuse these words:
He writes *well* (not *good*).   The apple tastes *good.* (See 289)
When it means "not sick," *well* is an adjective:
I am glad he is *well* again.

330 Do not use these nonstandard, dialectal adverbial expressions: *anywheres, nowheres, somewheres, nowhere near, illy, muchly.*

331 When *very* or *too* modifies a past participle (201), it should be accompanied by another adverb, such as *greatly* or *much.*
John was very *much* excited.
♦ The adverb *very* is overused as an intensifier and should be avoided. V*ery excited* is colloquially acceptable.

332 Do not use such words as *up* and *of* unnecessarily:
Let's *connect* (not *connect up*) these wires.
They lost all (not *all of*) their money.

333 *Kind of* and *sort of* should not be misused for such adverbs as *rather* and *somewhat*, when this is the meaning intended:
She was *somewhat* (not *sort of*) surprised.

334 Do not use *some* as an adverb in careful writing. Use *somewhat*:
He is *somewhat* better today.

335 *Thisaway* and *thataway* are dialectal forms:

Dialectal: The robbers went *thataway*.

Standard: The robbers went *that way*.

336 Do not use two negatives to express one negative idea; for example, do not use *not* with *hardly, scarcely, only, neither, never, no one, nobody, nothing, no,* or *none*:

There was *no one* at home.

As a rule, place *not* directly before the word it modifies:

Not every soldier can be a general.

Some apparently double negatives are correct:

She was not *unwilling* to help.	*No one* liked the play, *not* even Jane.

337 Use *from* after *different* and *differently* (361):

He thinks differently *from* (not *than*) you.

338 Do not use any word between the parts of an infinitive (199, 235) if it results in an awkward expression:

Awkward: He told me to *not* sell the book.

Correct: He told me *not* to sell the book.

339 Do not misuse the adjective *easy* for the adverb *easily*:

We can finish *easily* (not *easy*) by noon.

♦ Certain phrases, such as *take it easy, go easy,* are colloquially acceptable.

340 The position of the adverb is rather flexible in English sentences, but sometimes the position of an adverb will change the meaning of a sentence:

He *only* seems interested in reading. (He is really not interested.)

He seems interested *only* in reading. (Reading is apparently his only interest.)

Prepositions

341 A preposition (44) is a word or a word group that shows the relation between its object (106) and some other word in the sentence:

The eagle soared *above* the peak. (*Above* is a preposition; *peak* is the object of the preposition. The two together form a prepositional phrase.)

♦ A word ordinarily used as a preposition may be used as a simple adverb (316, 318) when it has no object, or it may become part of a verb:

We have met *before*. (**adverb**)

John arrived *before* dinner. (**preposition**)

Send *in* the applicant. Send the applicant *in*. He was sent *in*. (**adverb**)

342 Although prepositions are variously classified, it is sufficient to know four general classes: simple, compound, participial, and phrasal.

343 A simple preposition is made up of one word: *by, for, in, with, on.*

344 A compound preposition is made up of two words used as one: *without, upon, into, before, inside.*

345 A participial preposition is the present participle of certain verbs used with the function of a preposition: *regarding, excepting, respecting, barring.*

346 A phrasal preposition·is a phrase used as a preposition: *in spite of, in accordance with, with regard to, from below, over against.*

347 Some of the words most frequently used as prepositions are *aboard, about, above, across, after, against, along, amid, among, around, at, before, behind, below, beneath, beside, between, beyond, by, down, during, except, for, from, from among, from between, from under, in, into, of, off, on, out of, outside, over, round, round about, since, through, throughout, to, unto, under, underneath, up, upon, with,* and *within.*

348 A preposition and its object (with the modifiers of the object) form a phrase (8) which has the use of an adjective (275) when it modifies a noun or a pronoun, and the use of an adverb (316) when it modifies a verb, adjective, or an adverb:

The tree *in the park* is an oak. (adjective phrase modifying *tree*)
We walked *beside the river.* (adverb phrase modifying *walked*)

♦ Some linguists state that a prepositional phrase may be used as a noun (47, 61). The following is an example:

At the door was where he left them.

Usage

349 There are some two hundred and eighty-four words and phrases in English used as prepositions and prepositional phrases. The following sections (350–364) illustrate a number of the distinctions to be made in correct usage. Modern dictionaries carefully indicate the idiomatic distinctions to be made in formal expression.

350 One may *agree to* a thing and *agree with* a person:
I *agree* to the plan.   You *agree* with me.

351 One may be *angry at* or *about* a thing and *angry with* a person:
I was *angry at* the discourtesy.   He was *angry with* me.

352 One *arrives in* a large city, *at* a small place:
He *arrived in* Chicago.   We *arrived at* the village.

353 *Besides* means *in addition to; beside* means *by the side of:*
There were two boys *besides* Henry.   He sat *beside* me.

354 *Between* refers to two; *among,* to more than two:
>She divided the candy *between* the two boys.
>He threw the confetti *among* the crowd.

355 One is *accompanied by* a person, *with* a thing:
>Mabel was *accompanied by* her mother.
>The rain was *accompanied with* hail.

356 Do not use *inside of* for *within:*
>He did not work *within* (not *inside of*) a week.

357 *Into* denotes entrance; *in* denotes location:
>He jumped *into* the water.　　　He swam *in* the river.

358 One may die *of* disease, *from* exposure, or *by* violence:
>He died *of* pneumonia.　　　She died *from* exposure, not *by* her
>　　　　　　　　　　　　　　own act.

359 *By* is the word to use after *follow* when referring to what follows:
>The murderer was followed *by* a mob.

360 *Differ with* means *disagree in opinion; differ from* means *be unlike* or *dissimilar:*
>I *differ with* you about the value of the painting.
>The horses *differ from* each other in color.

361 *From* should be used with the adjective *different:*
>This hat is different *from* (not *than*) that. (337)

362 One *parts from* a person, *with* a thing:
>Romeo *parted from* Juliet.
>The miser did not wish to *part with* his gold.

363 Do not use *in back of* for *behind:*
>The garage is *behind* (not *in back of*) the house.

364 Do not use unnecessary words such as: accept *of,* off *of,* remember *of,* where *at,* where *to.*

Conjunctions

365 A **conjunction** (45) connects words or groups of words; in form it may be a single word or a group of words:
>Robert *and* James are here. (a single word connecting two words)
>She came *while* you were away. (a single word connecting clauses)
>The teachers *as well as* the students had a good time. (a group of words used as a conjunction)

366 Although conjunctions have many classifications, it is sufficient for our purpose to note only three general classes: **coordinating, subordinating,** and **correlative.**

Relative adverbs used as conjunctions are also called **conjunctive adverbs** or **adverbial conjunctions.**

367 A **coordinating conjunction** connects two words, two phrases, or two clauses of equal rank:

Paul *and* Carl are here. (*And* connects two nouns.)

She liked to read *but* not to write (not *writing*). (*But* connects two infinitives.)

The coordinating conjunctions in most general use include *and, but, for, or, nor, yet.* The conjunctive adverbs, such as *however, then, therefore,* and *thus,* also connect independent clauses (320).

368 A **subordinating conjunction** connects two clauses of unequal rank; that is, it joins a dependent (subordinate) clause (398) to the independent clause (397) on which it depends:

I was here *before* you came.

Some of the subordinating conjunctions are *as, as if, because, before, if, since, that, till, unless, when, where, whether.*

The relative pronouns *who, whom, whose, which, what, that,* also serve as subordinating conjunctions (135).

369 Conjunctions that are used in pairs are called **correlative conjunctions** and include *both-and, either-or, neither-nor, not only-but also.*

Neither John *nor* I will be able to come.

Usage

370 Do not use *except* for *unless:*

We will play *unless* (not *except* or *without*) you object.

371 Do not use *without* for *that:*

I never meet her *that I do not* (not *without I*) admire her wit.

372 Do not use *like* for *as, as if, as though,* or *that* in formal writing:

Walk *as* (not *like*) he told you.

It seems *that* (not *like*) he should help.

373 *And etc.* for *etc.* is incorrect. *Etc.* is an abbreviation of the Latin words *et cetera,* meaning *and so forth;* therefore *and* is not needed.

374 *And, but,* and *or* are used so frequently that a piece of writing may soon become overloaded with compound sentences. Learn to use the other conjunctions for sentence variety.

375 *And, or, but,* and correlative conjunctions (369) should be used to join expressions that are parallel in form:

She liked *to stroll* on the beach and *to watch* the sea birds.

He is coming *with us* by car or *with his family* by train.

376 Most grammarians agree that the relative (conjunctive pronoun) *which* should not be used to refer to an entire clause (166):

Questionable: The traffic was heavy, *which* caused me to be late.

Better: I was late because the traffic was heavy.

377 When a subordinate conjunction (368) introduces two or more statements of equal importance, the conjunction should in most cases be repeated before each clause to make the meaning clear:

She told me *that* she had won the prize and *that* she would return.

378 *Nor* is used with *neither* or after some negative word:

He can *neither* read *nor* (not *or*) write.

He cannot dive, *nor* does he like to swim.

379 After verbs of *saying, thinking,* and *feeling,* do not use *as* to replace *that:*

I feel *that* (not *as*) I should not go.

380 Do not use *where* for *that:*

I read in the paper *that* (not *where*) the price of wheat had advanced.

381 Do not use *if* for *whether* in formal writing:

I do not know *whether* (not *if*) he will come.

382 Each of a pair of correlative conjunctions (369) should be placed immediately before the word it connects:

He eats *both* meat *and* fish. (not: He *both* eats meat *and* fish.)

383 In clauses of purpose, do not use *so* for *so that* in formal use:

He worked hard so *that* he could pay his debts.

384 Use *when* to follow *scarcely* or *hardly;* use *than* to follow the expression of a comparison:

He had scarcely started *when* the accident happened.

He did better *than* I expected.

385 Use *that* before a clause which follows a verb of *saying, thinking,* or *feeling* when the verb is followed by an infinitive:

He studied hard, for he knew *that* to fail would be his ruin.

386 Do not omit *as* when it is necessary to complete a comparison:

Illogical: Jane is tall, if not taller than you.

Logical: Jane is *as* tall *as* you, if not taller.

3

The Sentence

It has been well said that good English is lucid English. If this be true, then the speaker or writer who has mastered the English sentence in its simple and in its complex forms will have the means of self-expression with clarity and precision. In modern terms, one communicates.

Just as a carpenter studies the materials and tools in order to best build a house, we study the sentence as the tool of effective expression for our thoughts.

Sentence Structure and Analysis

387 A sentence must express a thought (1); therefore it must have a subject and a predicate (3, 4) either expressed or understood (5); and it may also have modifiers (7) and independent elements (12).

388 In general sentences are made up of **words, phrases** (8), and **clauses** (9). The classification of words has been given in Chapter Two under *Parts of Speech*. Phrases and clauses are also classified in several ways.

389 A **phrase** is a group of related words used as a part of a sentence but not having a subject (3) or a predicate (4). A phrase may be a modifier (7, 8), a connective (365), or a substantive (47):

Ann came *with me.* (modifier)

To make a mistake is not disgraceful. (substantive)

The **verb phrase** (15, 41, 181, 391) is not a modifier, a connective, nor a substantive.

390 According to **structure** there are four general classes of phrases: **prepositional, infinitive, participial,** and **gerund:**

   1. A **prepositional phrase** includes a preposition (341, 347) and its object and modifiers of the object:

      Burns lived *among the hills.*

   2. An **infinitive phrase** includes an infinitive and its object or complement and modifiers:

      Byron liked *to write poetry.*

   3. A **participial phrase** includes a participle and its object and modifiers:

      The girl, *walking quickly,* joined the others.

   4. A **gerund phrase** includes a gerund and its object and modifiers:

      Painting beautiful pictures is interesting work.

391 The **verb phrase** is a phrasal verb, that is, a verb consisting of two or more words (41). The various forms of *be, have* and of the auxiliary verbs (*can, may, shall, will, must, ought, do*) are combined with main verb forms to make up the verb phrase.

392 According to their **use** phrases are classified as follows: **noun** (substantive), **adjective,** and **adverb.** They are referred to by some writers as **nominal, adjectival, adverbial.**

393 A **noun phrase** may be used as a regular noun, with the exception that it is never used in the possessive case (116):

   Playing tennis is delightful exercise. (This is a gerund phrase, 390-4, used as the subject. All gerunds are, of course, used as nouns, 200.)

   The following sentences illustrate other uses of gerunds as nouns:

   My favorite exercise is *swimming.* (**predicate nominative, 96**)

   Robert likes *swimming.* (**object of verb, 102**)

   We talked about *swimming.* (**object of a preposition, 106**)

   Her work, *writing stories,* is very interesting. (**apposition with the subject, 100, 101**)

   He likes his work, *teaching music.* (**apposition with object of verb**)

   The infinitive phrase (390-2) has the following uses as a noun:

   To try is noble. (**subject**)

   I like *to swim.* (**direct object**)

   Her desire is *to succeed.* (**predicate nominative**)

   Her aim, *to succeed,* is worthy. (**apposition with subject**)

   I dread my task, *to sell tickets.* (**apposition with object of verb**)

   He spoke of his duty, *to work.* (**apposition with object of preposition**)

The prepositional phrase (390-1, 348) is not regularly used as a noun, but some writers consider the following as an example of such a use:

Over the fence is out.

♦ The participial phrase (390-3) is used as an adjective and not as a noun; but the gerund is in reality a form of participle used as a noun and is sometimes called **verbal noun** or **participial noun** (56, 200).

394 An **adjective phrase** is a phrase used as an adjective (42, 275-290, 399). The prepositional phrase (390-1), the infinitive phrase (390-2), or the participial phrase (390-3) may be used as an adjective:

The house *on the hill* is white. (**prepositional phrase** used as an adjective to modify *house*)

Evelyn has a great deal of work *to do*. (**infinitive phrase** used as an adjective to modify *work*)

The girl *holding the bat* is Susan. (**participial phrase** used as an adjective to modify *girl*)

395 An **adverb phrase** is a phrase used as an adverb (43, 316–326, 413). Phrases used as adverbs are generally either prepositional or infinitive:

Helen came *with Mary*. (**prepositional phrase** used as an adverb to modify *came*)

The men came *to work*. (**infinitive phrase** used as an adverb to modify *came*)

♦ A phrase may sometimes be either adverbial or adjectival:

He saw a book *on the table*.   He knew the book *on the table*.

396 A **clause** is a group of words which contains a subject (3) and a predicate (4). It is usually considered a part of a sentence; but when it is capable of standing alone, it is equivalent to a simple sentence (21). Words are sometimes properly omitted from the clause (10):

Mary is the girl *who wrote the letter*.

The officer said, "*Stop*." (*You*, the **subject**, is omitted here.)

Clauses as parts of a sentence are classified as **independent** (called also **principal clause** or **main clause**) and **dependent** or **subordinate**.

397 The **independent clause** is one that makes complete sense when standing alone and that is grammatically complete.

The students deliver papers before they come to school. (The clause *The students deliver papers* could stand alone, as it expresses a complete thought.)

398 A **dependent** (subordinate) **clause** is used as a part of speech in a sentence and usually does not make sense when standing alone:

The students deliver papers *before they come to school.* (The clause *before they come to school* is incomplete in sense when standing alone; here it is used as an adverb and modifies the verb in the main clause.)

399 A dependent clause may be used as a **noun,** an **adjective,** or an **adverb.** The **noun clause** may be used in a variety of ways. These uses are illustrated in sections 400–407. **Adjective** clauses and **adverb** clauses are explained in sections 408 and 409.

Noun Clause

400 The noun clause is used as subject (3) of a sentence:

What she thought seemed important to him.

401 The noun clause is used as direct object of a verb (6):

Don said *that he tried.*

♦ An infinitive (199) construction which often replaces a *that* clause is sometimes called an **infinitive clause:**

John asked *me to stay.* (This is equivalent to *John asked that I should stay;* therefore *me to stay* is a noun clause, of which *me* is the subject—the subject of an infinitive is always in the objective case—and *to stay* is the predicate. *Me to stay* is the direct object of *asked.*)

402 The noun clause is used as object of a preposition (106):

We talked about *what we would do.*

403 The noun clause is used as predicate nominative (96):

The fact is *that she won the prize.*

404 The noun clause is used in apposition (100) with the subject:

The report *that she won is correct.*

405 The noun clause is used in apposition (101) with the object of a verb:

You made the statement *that she won.*

406 The noun clause is used in apposition with object of a preposition:

We thought of his answer, *"I do not care what you say."*

407 The noun clause is used in apposition (100) with the predicate nominative:

The clearest evidence is the fact *that she won.*

Adjective Clause

408 An **adjective clause** is a clause used as an adjective (275, 414). The adjective clause may be introduced by a relative pronoun (135), a relative adverb (such as *where, when, while, why*) or a subordinate conjunction (368). The relative adverbs are also classed as subordinating conjunctions, but when used to introduce adjective clauses,

they have antecedents. In some instances, the word which connects the clause is omitted:

This is the book *that I bought.* (adjective clause, modifying *book*, introduced by the pronoun *that*)

That is the place *where we saw him.* (adjective clause, modifying *place*, introduced by the relative adverb *where*)

Is that the girl *we met yesterday?* (adjective clause omitting the introductory pronoun)

♦ Whether the introductory word is expressed or not, it must be considered as a part of the clause. The omitted word in the last example is *whom,* and it must be considered the object of *met.*

Adverb Clause

409 An **adverb clause** is a clause used as an adverb (316–326, 414). The adverb clause is introduced by a subordinating conjunction (368):

When we had finished our difficult task, we drove through the park. (The subordinating conjunction *when* introduces the adverb clause which modifies the verb *drove.*)

The adverb clause which stands at the beginning of a sentence is followed by a comma (497) unless it is very short and cannot be misread. A comma is usually not used when the main clause (397) stands first:

When we had finished our difficult task, we drove through the park.

After we left the lights were turned on.

We stayed at home *because the weather was unpleasant.* (The subordinating conjunction *because* introduces the adverb clause which modifies the verb *stayed.*)

Sentence Form

410 A sentence (1,387) must have a subject and a predicate (2) and it may have other parts, such as objects, complements, and modifiers of all types (1–19). As to form, a sentence may be classified as **simple** (21), **compound** (22), **complex** (23), and **compound–complex** (20, 416). The **simple sentence** must have but one independent clause (397). The subject (3) or the predicate (4) or both (19) may be compound; and it may contain any number of phrases, but no dependent clause (398):

The man at the window sent a ticket for John. (This simple sentence contains two phrases.)

John and Melba bought baseballs and bats and packed them in cartons (This simple sentence contains a compound subject, a compound predicate, a compound direct object, and one phrase.)

Although there are certain parts (2) necessary to every sentence, all sentences are made up of words and groups of words. We have noted the classification of words as parts of speech (38–386) and the classification of groups of words as phrases and clauses (389–409). In the study of the relationships of the parts of the sentence, there are three methods used by grammarians—parsing, analyzing, diagramming—to state or show these relationships.

411 **Parsing a word** is to name the part of speech (38–52) to which it belongs, its modifications, and its construction in the sentence, that is, to give a grammatical description of it:

Mary paints beautiful pictures.

Mary is a proper noun (55), feminine gender (65), third person (72), singular number (74), nominative case (95), subject of the verb *paints*.

Paints is a regular transitive verb (171, 174), indicative mood (187), present tense (191), active voice (184), third person (72), singular number (74) to agree (197) with its subject *Mary*.

Beautiful is a descriptive adjective (279), positive degree (292), and modifies the noun *pictures*.

Pictures is a common noun (54), neuter gender (66), third person (72), plural number (75), objective case (102), object of the verb *paints*.

412 **Analyzing a sentence** is to state the relation of the parts of the sentence to each other:

The little child liked the roses in the garden.

This is a simple declarative sentence (21, 25).

The *little child* is the complete subject (14); *child* is the simple subject (13); *the* and *little* are adjectives modifying *child*. *Liked the roses in the garden* is the complete predicate (16); *liked*, the simple predicate (15), is completed by the object *roses* (102). The object (6) is modified by the adjective *the* and the adjective phrase (394) *in the garden*.

413 **Diagramming a sentence** is to make a visual picture of the word relationships in it. Other diagrams of the simple sentence are given under 4, 6, 7, 19, 96, 100, 105, 179, 265, 266, 269.

DIAGRAM—A simple sentence (21) with *a prepositional phrase* (390-1) used as an adjective (394):

The book *on the desk* is blue.

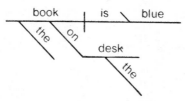

DIAGRAM—A simple sentence with *a prepositional phrase* used as an adverb (395):

A dog ran *under the fence.*

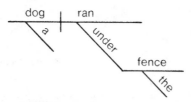

414 A **complex sentence** (23) has but **one** independent clause (397) and one or more dependent clauses (398):

Ruth left *when I arrived.* (*Ruth left* is an **independent clause.** *When I arrived* is a **dependent clause** which modifies the verb *left* as an adverb, 409.)

This is the girl *who wrote the story that won the prize.* (*This is the girl* is an independent clause. (*Who wrote the story* is a **dependent clause** that modifies the noun *girl* as an adjective, 408. *That won the prize* is a **dependent clause** that modifies *story* as an adjective.)

The analysis of a complex sentence is similar to that of the simple sentence:

Bob saw the girl who wrote the story. (This is a complex sentence. *Bob saw the girl* is the main, or independent, clause, of which *Bob* is the subject, *saw* is the verb, and *girl* is the direct object. The dependent clause is *who wrote the story; who* is the subject of the dependent clause, *wrote* is the verb, and *story* is the direct object. The dependent clause is an adjective (408), and it modifies the noun *girl.*)

DIAGRAM—A complex sentence with an *adjective clause* (408) introduced by a *relative pronoun* (135) used as *object:*

I saw the horse *which you bought.*

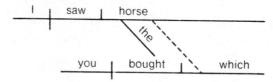

DIAGRAM—A complex sentence with an *adjective clause* introduced by a *relative pronoun* (135) used as *subject*:

The girl *who sat beside me* is my cousin.

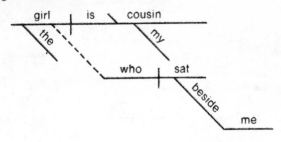

DIAGRAM—A complex sentence with an *adjective clause* introduced by a *relative adverb* (408):

That is the place *where we saw the deer*.

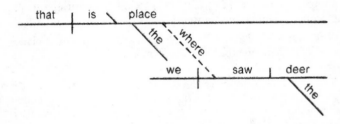

DIAGRAM—A complex sentence with an *adverb clause* (409) introduced by the *subordinating conjunction* (368) *if*:

He will win *if we help him*.

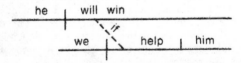

DIAGRAM—A complex sentence with an *adverb clause* introduced by the *subordinating conjunction* (368) *when*:

Mother met us *when we arrived*.

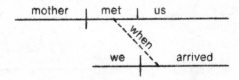

DIAGRAM—A complex sentence with a *noun clause* used as *subject* (400):

That you succeed is the truth.

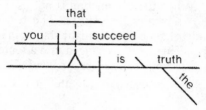

DIAGRAM—A complex sentence with a *noun clause* used as the *object* of a verb (401):

My mother said *that he had won the prize.*

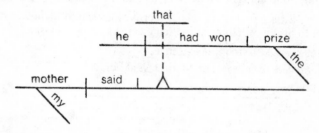

DIAGRAM—A complex sentence with a *noun clause* used as *predicate nominative* or *subjective complement* (403):

The truth is *that he bought the house.*

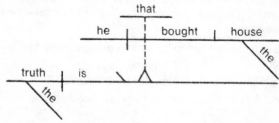

415 A **compound sentence** (22) has **two** or **more** independent clauses (397) joined by conjunctions (365-369) or by punctuation (489, 495) or by both:

The little girl went to school, but her brother stayed at home.

The short, friendly little girl went to school; but her brother stayed at home.

The little girl went to school; her brother stayed at home.

When there are no other commas (first example) used in a compound sentence a comma is placed before the conjunction (495). But when one is used, then the comma is replaced by the semicolon (second example). When the conjunction is not used (third example), a semicolon (489) separates the clauses. The two clauses of the sentence, being independent (397), might stand alone as sentences. But when an independent clause is changed into a sentence, it ceases to be a clause, for a clause by definition is a part of a sentence:

The little girl went to school. Her brother stayed at home. (two simple sentences)

The compound sentence is analyzed in the same way as simple sentences except that the connecting words are mentioned. Every independent clause is practically equivalent to a simple sentence, and a compound sentence may have any number of independent clauses:

The little girl went to school; her brother stayed at home; her father went to his office. (three clauses connected by semicolons, 489)

DIAGRAM—A *compound* sentence:

John goes to college, but Mark stays at home.

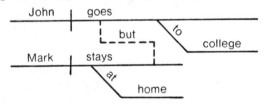

416 If either independent clause of a compound sentence has a subordinate clause (398), the sentence is called **compound–complex** or **complex–compound:**

When Henry lost the race, he was disappointed; but he was not discouraged.

DIAGRAM—A *compound–complex* sentence:

He lost the knife that he bought, but he may find it.

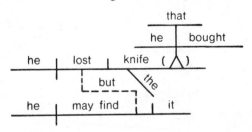

Sentence Style

417 Sentences are also classified as to the arrangement of their material as **periodic, loose,** and **balanced.**

418 A **periodic sentence** is one in which the main thought is not given until the end of the sentence is reached. This type of sentence is not grammatically complete until the last word. It lends emphasis:

Today, as never before in the history of the world, we need leadership.

♦ A compound sentence as a whole cannot be periodic, but its parts may be periodic.

419 A **loose sentence** gives the main thought and then adds details. It is the rambling type of expression, much used in conversation:

Lancelot returned with Guinevere in the spring when the flowers were in bloom and the world seemed full of gladness.

420 A **balanced sentence** has two parts which are alike in construction. The thoughts in the two parts may be either in agreement or in contrast:

He told his story at home, then he repeated it at school.

He was always industrious, but he was never successsful.

Variety

421 **Variety in Sentence Structure**   One form of sentence may be just as effective as another, but any form becomes monotonous when it is used too frequently. Valuable practice can be had by expressing similar ideas in sentences of different form:

1. **Simple:** Mary Jones, the efficient president of our class, is an excellent musician. (An appositive, 101, is used.)

2. **Complex:** Mary Jones, who is the efficient president of our class, is an excellent musician. (A dependent, 398, nonrestrictive clause, 499, is used.)

3. **Compound** with a conjunction (415): Mary Jones is the efficient president of our class, and she is also an excellent musician. (A comma, 495, precedes the conjunction.)

4. **Compound** without a conjunction (415): Mary Jones is the efficient president of our class; she is also an excellent musician. (A semicolon, 489, separates the independent clauses.)

5. **Compound–complex** (416): Mary Jones, who is the president of our class, is a very efficient officer; and she is also an excellent musician. (For punctuation, see 489, 491.)

6. **Two simple sentences** (410): Mary Jones is the efficient president of our class. She is also a very good musician.

7. Three simple sentences: Mary Jones is the president of our class. She is a very efficient officer. She is also an excellent musician. (Short sentences give emphasis to expresssion, but they tend to become monotonous, 449.)

422 VARIETY IN STRUCTURE PATTERNS Through variety in structure patterns, sentences may be kept free from monotony:

1. Phrase (390-3): *Finishing the job*, the people left.
2. Phrase (390-3): *Having finished the job*, the people left.
3. Clause (398): *The people who had finished the job* left.
4. Clause (408): *When the people finished the job*, they left.
5. Absolute construction (99): *The job being finished*, the people left.
6. Absolute construction (99): *The job finished*, the people left.
7. Gerund (56, 200): *After finishing the job*, the people left.

◆ The use of the participial phrase (390-3) to replace the adjective clause (408) lends economy to and often strengthens the statement.

The person *standing beside the gate* is an officer. (phrase)
The person *who is standing beside the gate* is an officer. (clause)

423 VARIETY IN ARRANGEMENT In the arrangement of the material in sentences, there should be variety as to the place of emphasis. The periodic sentence (418) gives emphasis to the important idea in a sentence, but it should not be used either to the exclusion of the loose sentence (419) or, where appropriate, of the balanced sentence (420).

Yesterday afternoon about four o'clock my friend met with a serious accident. (periodic sentence)
My friend met with a serious accident yesterday afternoon about four o'clock. (loose sentence)

424 VARIETY IN LENGTH The length of sentences should be varied. Short sentences become tiresome when used to excess, and a sequence of long sentences has a tendency to make reading more difficult.

425 VARIETY OF BEGINNING Sentences which begin in the normal order (29) of subject first may become as tedious as any other oft-repeated sentence form; therefore, variety of beginning is important in gaining the reader's attention. The following beginnings suggest various ways of attaining variety.

426 A sentence may begin with a prepositional phrase (390-1):
In those days people loved dangerous adventure.

427 A sentence may begin with a participial phrase (390-3):

Hoping to reach home before the storm, the rider urged his horse forward.

The day being clear, we played tennis. (**absolute, 99**)

428 A sentence may begin with an adverb (316):

Silently and sadly the old man turned away.

A sentence may begin with an adjective (275):

Beautiful as the trees were, they were cut down for the new building.

429 A sentence may begin with a direct object of a verb (102):

Friends and *enemies* alike he betrayed in order that he might gain wealth.

430 A sentence may begin with a dependent clause (398):

That you are in earnest will help your cause. (**noun, 400**)

When the time comes, we will act. (**adverb, 409**)

431 A sentence may begin with a verb (41) or verbal (198):

Work hard if you wish to succeed.

To succeed is the desire of nearly everyone. (**infinitive phrase, 390-2**)

Helping others gives real joy. (**gerund phrase, 390-4**)

Effectiveness

432 **Effective Sentences** An effective sentence must have **unity, coherence,** and **emphasis.**

433 **Unity** requires that the sentence must express connected thoughts; hence the relationship of thoughts must be clearly shown:

Weak: Fred Smith visited me last summer, and he once lived in England.

Better: Fred Smith, who visited me last summer, once lived in England.

434 **Coherence** requires that the connections between different parts of the sentence be made perfectly clear:

Confusing: Ruth returned the book which she had borrowed last week this afternoon.

Clear: This afternoon Ruth returned the book which she had borrowed last week.

435 **Emphasis,** or force, is given to the main ideas of a sentence by placing them properly in the position of greatest emphasis—the beginning and the close. Force is given by arranging ideas in order of climax, by repetition of words or sounds, by the use of figures of speech (676), by the addition of modifiers (275, 316), as well as by conciseness of expression and by variety (421–431):

1. Emphasis gained by **position:**

   Poor: After a long search they found the lost child finally in the woods.
   Better: After a long search in the woods they found the lost child.

2. Emphasis gained by **climax:**

   Flood has brought to these people hunger, disease, death. (See **anti-climax,** 458)

3. Emphasis gained by **repetition:**

   Mr. Smith is a man who is loyal—*loyal* to his friends, *loyal* to his family, *loyal* to his co-workers.

   ♦ The repetition of the same beginning letter or sound, called *alliteration,* is used effectively in advertising: *w*atch, *w*ait, *w*in.

4. Emphasis gained by **figures of speech:**

   a. **Simile** (677): The oak stood *like a sentinel.*
   b. **Metaphor** (678, 679): The rose is *queen* of all flowers.
   c. **Personification** (680): The trees *laughed* in the June sunlight.
   d. **Hyperbole** (681): He gave a *thousand* excuses for his failure.

5. Emphasis gained by **addition of modifiers** (275, 316):

   He is a *handsome, intelligent, ambitious* young man.

436 A more **concise expression** sometimes adds force. Conciseness in statement may be gained by changes in form or style:

1. An appositive (101) may be substituted for a sentence:
   Susan Smith addressed the meeting. *She is our president.*
   Susan Smith, *our president,* addressed the meeting.

2. A participial phrase (394) may replace a clause (396)
   The man *who is standing near the desk* is the president.
   The man *standing near the desk* is the president.

   A participial phrase also may be used to replace a sentence:

   The beautiful building was destroyed by fire. *It was completed only a year ago.*

   The beautiful building, *completed only a year ago,* was destroyed by fire.

3. A noun clause (400–407) may replace a sentence:
   Anita is ambitious. *That fact is self-evident.*
   That Anita is ambitious is self-evident.

4. A gerund may make a sentence more concise (200, 266):
   It is my ambition to achieve a deserved success.
   The *achieving* of a deserved success is my ambition.

5. An infinitive may make a sentence more concise (199, 265):

That I may win a deserved success is my ambition.
To win a deserved success is my ambition.

Structure and Style

437 CONFUSING REFERENCES A sentence may be faulty because a pronoun is placed where it may refer to more than one word: There should be *no uncertainty* as to *what word* is *the antecedent* (129) of *a pronoun.*

438 Confusing reference of the relative pronoun:

Confusing: She left the book on the table which she had just bought from the publisher. (The *which* seems to refer to *table*, though it should refer to *book*.)

Clear: She left on the table the book which she had just bought from the publisher. (The *which* clearly refers to *book*.)

439 Confusing reference of the personal pronoun:

Confusing: Harry told Fred that he would become a great musician. (It is not clear whether *he* refers to Harry or to Fred.)

Clear: Harry said to Fred, "You will become a great musician." OR, Harry said to Fred, "I will become a great musician."

440 An indefinite antecedent (129) of the pronoun:

Confusing: She asked me to help him, but I forgot about it. (The *it* has nothing definite to refer to.)

Clear: She made a request that I help him, but I forgot about it. (The antecedent is *request*.)

441 As a rule avoid using *which* to refer to a clause (166, 376):

Ineffective: My uncle came to see me, which pleased me greatly.
Better: I was pleased because my uncle came to see me.

442 Do not misuse *them* for *those:*

I think those (not *them*) roses are lovely.

Do not use *they* with indefinite reference (169):

People (not *They*) say he is honest.

443 UNRELATED IDEAS Unrelated ideas should not be placed in the same sentence:

Disconnected: Fred won the race, and he likes chocolate candy.

444 COMMA BLUNDER (*also comma splice* or *fault*) Two independent clauses (397) not joined by a conjunction should not be separated by a comma unless they make up a series (496). They should be separated by a semicolon (489) or written as two sentences:

Incorrect: We spent the summer in Colorado, we had a good time.
Correct: We spent the summer in Colorado, and we had a good time.
Correct: We spent the summer in Colorado; we had a good time.
Correct: We spent the summer in Colorado. We had a good time.

445 Run-on Sentences A serious and common writing error is the run-on sentence in which two sentences are written as one without punctuation (35):

Incorrect: We rambled through the woods all day we did not reach home till late.
Correct: We rambled through the woods all day. We did not reach home till late.

446 Period Fault Through the misuse of the period, students sometimes write fragments for sentences:

Incorrect: We returned home. Hoping to have another picnic soon. (A participial phrase (390-3) is written incorrectly as a sentence.)
Correct: We returned home, hoping to have another picnic soon.
Incorrect: They liked all kinds of games. Especially football.
Correct: They liked all kinds of games, especially football.
Incorrect: We had a good time. When we were in Colorado. (A dependent clause, 398, is written incorrectly as a sentence.)
Correct: We had a good time when we were in Colorado.

♦ Some professional writers occasionally do use the fragment very effectively in their work, but the young writer should construct complete sentences.

447 And–And Construction It sounds childlike to join many sentences by *and* as if all the ideas were of equal rank:

Childish: We finished our work, and we went fishing, and we had a good time.
Improved: After we had finished our work, we went fishing and had a good time.

448 Omission of Necessary Words This common fault occurs in several ways:

1. Subject of sentence omitted. The subject should be expressed in a declarative sentence (25) in order to make the meaning clear (33):

Faulty: Went to the football game yesterday.
Correct: I (*or* He, They, etc.) went to the football game yesterday.

In the imperative sentence (26) the subject is correctly omitted:
Correct: Lend me your book.

2. Subject of dependent clause omitted:

Not clear: When in Chicago, my father sent me a watch.
Correct: When I was (*or* he was) in Chicago, my father sent me a watch.
Not clear: When ten years old, his mother died.
Correct: When he was ten years old, his mother died.

In elliptical sentences (5) the omission (ellipsis) of words gives strength rather than weakness, especially in the answers to questions.

Welcome. (*You are* welcome.)
Where have I been? At school. (*I have been* at school.)
Do you like Shakespeare's plays? Yes. (Yes, *I like Shakespeare's plays.*)

449 PRIMER SENTENCES Some students fall into the habit of writing monotonous short sentences like those in a primer:

Childish: We went to town. We stayed all day. We came home. We were tired.
Better: After we had spent the day in town, we came home tired.

♦ Short sentences may at times be used effectively, as an element of style, for emphasis.

She planned. She worked. She succeeded.

450 PARALLEL STRUCTURE Parallel thoughts should be expressed in terms that are grammatically parallel:

Faulty: *Swimming* is more enjoyable than *to row*. (One is a gerund and the other is an infinitive.)
Better: *Swimming* is more enjoyable than *rowing*. (Both are gerunds, 200.)
Better: *To swim* is more enjoyable than *to row*. (Both are infinitives, 199.)

451 DANGLING MODIFIERS Modifiers should not be left dangling—with nothing to modify (271). A participial phrase (390-3) or a prepositional phrase (390-1) at the beginning of a sentence relates to the subject of that sentence. A participial phrase at the beginning of a sentence is followed by a comma:

Faulty: Walking down the street, the beautiful building was admired. (The *building* did no *walking*.)
Clear: Walking down the street, we admired the beautiful building.
Faulty: On entering the room, the picture is seen. (There is nothing for the phrase to modify; the *picture* does not do the *entering*.)
Clear: On entering the room, one may see the picture. (The introductory prepositional phrase which contains a gerund modifies *one*.)

452 MISPLACED MODIFIERS   Modifiers—whether they are words (340), phrases, or clauses—should be so placed that their meaning is immediately clear to the reader (438):

> **Confusing:** She almost spent a hundred dollars.
> **Clear:** She spent *almost* a hundred dollars.
> **Confusing:** We saw a man on a horse with a wooden leg.
> **Clear:** We saw a *man with a wooden* leg on a horse.
> **Confusing:** Jane saw a hat in a window which she liked. (438)
> **Clear:** Jane *saw in a window* a hat which she liked.

Shifts in Structure

453   Avoid needless shifts in **person:**

> One must work if *one* (not *you*) would succeed.

454   Avoid needless shifts in **number:**

> One should do *one's* (not *their*) duty.

455   Avoid needless shifts in **voice** (254, 255):

> As we went up the path, *we saw a snake* (not *a snake was seen*).

456   Avoid needless shifts in **tense:**

> The hunter went into the woods and there *he saw* (not *sees*) a deer.

457   Avoid needless shifts in **subject:**

> Ted's letters are interesting, because *they are cleverly written* (not *he is a clever boy*).

Loss of Sentence Effectiveness

458 ANTICLIMAX   The sentence may lose effectiveness from anticlimax, the reverse of climax (435-2), arranging ideas in the order of descending importance:

> Flood has brought to these people *death, disease, hunger.*

459 EFFECTIVE REPETITION   Repetition of words may either strengthen or weaken a composition, depending upon whether important or trivial ideas are repeated.

460   A sentence may be strengthened by repetition of important words or ideas (435-3)

461 MONOTONOUS REPETITION   Avoid the careless repetition of words:

> **Monotonous:** *Autumn* is the most *enjoyable* time of year, because it is in *autumn* that the weather is most *enjoyable.*

Improved: *Autumn* is the most *enjoyable* time of the year, because it is the season when the weather is most pleasant.

462 WORDINESS   A sentence may lose some of its effectiveness through wordiness—lack of economy in the use of words:

Wordy: He spoke in a very enthusiastic manner to the boys and girls of the high school about the wonderful opportunities of the future which lay ahead of them.

Concise: He spoke with enthusiasm to the high-school students about the opportunities of the future.

Redundancy denotes the use of unnecessary words:

Joe, he works fast.   This here book is good.

Tautology is the needless repetition of an idea in different words:

Refer it back to me.   It is an ancient, old castle.

463 ARTIFICIAL EXPRESSION   A sentence may lose in strength because of artificial expression:

Artificial: A vast concourse of those amicably inclined toward him assembled to do him honor on his natal day.

Natural: Many of his friends came to celebrate his birthday.

Mechanics
of Composition

One meaning of the word *mechanics* is "Routine procedure: technical details or method." It has been a long time since the advent of printing gave impetus to the standardization of the "technical details" of the English language as we use it today. In so complicated a structure as language, change, of course, is always taking place. But tradition dies slowly, and the usage reported here represents the standards of *American English* for our time. We should not forget that other sectors of the English-speaking world—Great Britain, Canada, Australia, South Africa, the West Indies, for example—may have come to accept usage patterns that vary from that of American usage.

Capitalization

464 Every sentence except a short parenthetical sentence within another should begin with a capital letter:

> The day was beautiful.
> Mary left yesterday (she had been here a week) for New York.

465 In traditional poetry every verse (line) begins with a capital:

> Poems are made by fools like me,
> But only God can make a tree.

> Some modern poets do not follow this rule.

466 The first word of a direct quotation in reported speech begins with a capital letter:

The girl said, "Wait for me."

467 The first word of a formal statement or resolution following introductory words (often italicized) is capitalized:

Resolved, That the world is growing better.

468 Every proper noun (55) (real or fictional) and every adjective derived from a proper noun (288) should be capitalized: *Boston, Bostonian, Spain, Spaniard; Samuel Johnson, Johnsonian; Miss Universe.*

469 The names of the days of the week, special holidays, and the names of the months are capitalized: *Sunday, Memorial Day, June.*

470 Names of the seasons are not capitalized ordinarily (483):

I like summer better than winter.

471 Names of particular associations and proper names resulting from membership in these associations are capitalized: *Republican Party, Republican; Democratic Party, Democrat; Methodist Church, Methodist; Garden Club; Vermont Historical Association.*

♦ Classes, schools, and colleges are capitalized when they refer to the particular:

John is a senior at Carlyle *College;* he attended Oak Hills *High School.*
The *Junior* Class invited Ms. Smith to speak.
The *Juniors* of 1972 came to the party; freshmen and sophomores were also invited.

472 Some abbreviations, such as the following, are written with capitals: A.D. (anno domini); B.C. (before Christ); SW (southwest); R.R. (railroad). Abbreviations of degrees and organizations are capitalized: A.B., M.D., Ph.D.; A.A.A., A.C.S., U.S.A.

♦ A wide variation exists in the use of upper and lower case in abbreviations, as well as in the use of the period (487), which tends to be dropped in current usage.

473 Important historical events, documents, buildings, and monuments should be capitalized:

Battle of Hastings, World War II, the Declaration of Independence, The White House, Lincoln Memorial.

474 The words *east, west, north,* and *south* are capitalized when they mean particular sections of a country, but they are not capitalized when they mean direction.

He came from the *South*. (**a section of a country**)

He went *south* from town. (**a direction**)

The compounds of these words follow the same rule:

He lives in the great *Northwest*.

Is Hutchinson *northwest* of Wichita?

475 The names of deities, religions, sacred documents are capitalized: *Allah, Jehovah, Brahma, Zeus, Buddhism, Shintoism, the Koran, the Bible.*

476 Nouns and personal pronouns (132) referring to God or to Christ are capitalized; but some writers do not capitalize the personal pronoun when its antecedent (129) is expressed:

I know *He* is the *Lord*.   Jesus loves *his* friends.

477 Names for the Bible and its parts and books begin with capital letters: *Bible, the Scriptures Old Testament, Deuteronomy.* (Do not italicize such words in running text.)

478 The first, last, and important words in the titles of books, literary articles, pictures, musical compositions, chapters of books, poems, plays, stories, newspapers, and magazines begin with capitals. Prepositions, articles, and conjunctions are usually not capitalized unless they begin the title, but prepositions of five or more letters may be capitalized; a preposition at the end of a title is capitalized. If an article begins the title of a magazine or newspaper, it is not capitalized unless it begins a sentence:

"Ode on a Grecian Urn"   He reads the *New York Times*.

479 The pronoun *I* and the vocative *O* (O Apollo) are always capitalized, but the interjection *oh* is capitalized only when it begins a sentence or stands alone:

Oh, will they come?   *Oh!*

480 The initials of a person's name are capitalized.

481 Titles used with proper names are capitalized:

We think that *Captain Smith* would make a good leader.

He saw *Principal John Moore* at the meeting.

482 When a civil or personal title is used as a proper noun referring to a specific person or thing, it is correct to capitalize it.

The *President* of our company was mentioned in the news.

Ann went with *Mother* and me to see her mother and father.

Will you help me, *Father*, with my work?

The *Secretary of State* will be named soon.

Our *Federal Government* differs from other federal governments.

483 Common nouns are capitalized when they are strongly personified:
Come, lovely *Spring,* and make us glad.

484 A common noun, such as *river, mountain, park, lake, gulf, ocean, street, avenue, hotel, church, school, club, society, or company,* is properly capitalized when it becomes a part of a particular name:
Is Lowell *School* near Belmont *Park?*
Does Clifton *Avenue* cross Maple *Street?*

Newspaper usage, although not all mass media follow it, shows some variation of this rule as in these examples:
Is Lowell school near Belmont park?
Does Clifton avenue cross Maple street?

But when the common noun precedes the particular name, it is capitalized even in the newspapers:
He lives near *Lake Erie.*

485 It is good practice to refer to a good dictionary for the capitalization of words as proper nouns and adjectives. Many words do have correct usage as both common (generic) and proper nouns: *renaissance–Renaissance, revolution–Revolution, ohm–Ohm, watt–Watt.*

Punctuation

Period

486 A period should be placed at the end of every declarative (25) and every imperative (26) sentence unless it is used as an exclamatory (28) sentence or in a sentence used parenthetically within another sentence (464). An elliptical expression (5, 448) used as a substitute for a sentence is followed by a period or other end punctuation:
Jean went to Europe last summer. (**declarative**)
Let me see your new book. (**imperative**)
Annette Jones (she is president of our class) will preside. (**parenthetical sentence** with no capital, 464, and no period) Yes. (**elliptical**)

♦ The polite request expressed in interrogative form so frequent in letters is generally followed by a period, not a question mark (529):
Will you please send your latest catalog.

487 Use periods after a person's initials and some abbreviations (538):
Geo. F. Smith; A.D.; B.C.; A.M.; Mr.; Mrs.; Ms.

There are many exceptions, such as *IQ, DDT.* Abbreviations of many organization names omit periods: *WAFS, WAVES*—especially if they may be pronounced as a word (an acronym)—or they may be written either way:

Y.M.C.A. or *YMCA, USMC* or *U.S.M.C.*

Consult the dictionary as a guide to the handling of abbreviations. Do not use a period after a contraction or after a shortened form of a name used as a part of a whole name:

Ben Brown *isn't* here.

Only one period is necessary at the end of a sentence even when it ends with an abbreviation, but a question mark (529) may follow the period used after an abbreviation at the end of a sentence:

A great battle was fought in the year 490 B.C.

What battle was fought in the year 490 B.C.? (Marathon)

What great siege occurred in A.D. 490? (Ravenna)

488 Three periods are used to show omission in quoted material:

"He did his best . . . yet he never quite succeeded."

A fourth period is used at the end of a sentence.

Four periods show that a whole sentence (or sentences) has been omitted:

"He said they would come. . . . But they never did come."

The period is used between the integral and decimal parts of a mixed fraction and between figures indicating dollars and cents:

The lake is 62.35 miles long. One mile is 1.609 kilometers.

With the discount it will cost $14.22.

Semicolon

489 Use a semicolon between two clauses of a compound sentence (415) when they are not joined by a conjunction (365–369), unless they are very short and are used informally (496).

The rain fell in torrents; we turned everywhere for shelter. (This may be also stated as two sentences.)

He came, he saw, he went away.

490 The semicolon is used between clauses of a compound sentence which are joined by conjunctive adverbs (320), such as *therefore, hence, however, nevertheless, accordingly, thus, then:*

The day was very cold; therefore, we did not go for a ride.

491 The semicolon is properly used between clauses which are joined by conjunctions if the clauses are long, or when the clauses have internal commas:

John arrived last night, I am told; but because his plane was late, he could not come to the party.

♦ The semicolon is often used to prevent misreading:

We invited Cindy Webb, the captain of the team; Don Mills, the president of our class; and Joe Wynn, the chairperson of our group.

492 The semicolon usually precedes *as, namely,* or *thus* when used to introduce examples (for a single example a comma suffices):

Four boys were mentioned; *namely,* Henry, Manuel, David, and Clyde.

Only one color was used, *namely,* blue.

Colon

493 The colon is used to introduce formally a word, a list, examples, a statement or question, a series of statements, or a long quotation. An expression such as *the following* often precedes the list:

The following fruits are for sale: apples, peaches, pears.

494 A colon is used after the salutation of a business letter and is used between the parts of a number denoting time:

Dear Sir or Madam: The plane arrives at 6:15 A.M.

Comma

495 The general rule is that a comma is used between the clauses of a compound sentence (415) when they are joined by such conjunctions as *but, for, or, and.* Use the comma with *but* (unless the subject is the same); use the comma with *for* (and when needed to show it is not a preposition); use the comma with *or* (when the subject shifts); use the comma with *and* (unless the subject is closely connected in thought). If, however, the clauses are long or have commas within them, a semicolon should be used to separate them (see 491).

Robert entered the race, but he did not win.

Robert entered the race but did not win.

Robert sent them a letter, for he had to know.

Robert told them where to look, for he knew.

Robert was happy or he thought he was.

Robert was happy, or we would not have found him.

Robert dressed carefully, and on the way out he spoke to his father.

Robert dressed carefully and he wore his best suit.

496 Very short clauses making up a series and not joined by conjunctions may be separated by commas (489, 504):

She came, she looked, she went away.

497 An adverbial clause (409) which precedes a main clause (397), unless it is very short, is set off by a comma:

When my cousin came to spend the day with me, she found me at work.

If you expect to succeed, you must prepare yourself.

The comma is usually omitted when the adverbial clause follows the main clause.

My cousin found me at work when she came to spend the day with me.

498 A comma should be used to set off *yes* or *no* used as mild interjections or as sentence adverbs:

Yes, you may go.

Other mild interjections (46), such as *ah, oh, well, why,* are set off by commas when exclamation marks would be too strong:

Ah, well, who can tell what may happen?

499 Nonrestrictive phrases and clauses should be set off from the rest of the sentence by a comma or commas. A nonrestrictive phrase or clause is a nonessential phrase or clause; that is, it is a phrase or a clause which can be omitted without changing the meaning of the main clause (sentences 2, 3, and 6 have a restrictive or limiting clause or phrase):

1. Edgar Allan Poe, who wrote "The Raven," was an American writer. (The clause *who wrote "The Raven"* is not necessary to the meaning of the main clause.)

2. Students who study will learn. (The clause *who study* is necessary to explain which students will learn.)

3. The girl who sells the tickets is an honor student. (*Who sells the tickets* is necessary to explain which girl is an honor student.)

4. Jane Gray, *who sells the concert tickets,* is a member of our class. (The clause is not necessary; it merely explains that the girl sells tickets.)

5. The boy, *seeing the clouds,* hurried home. (The phrase is not necessary to explain *boy.*

6. The girl *holding the flag* is Margaret. (The phrase is necessary to tell which girl is Margaret.)

7. *Wishing to see the parade,* we went to town early. (A participial phrase, 390-3, that stands at the beginning of a sentence is followed by a comma.)

8. *The task being done,* we went home. (absolute construction, 99)

Restrictive or limiting clauses or phrases are not set apart by punctuation.

500 Items of a parenthetical nature are set off by commas. Two commas are necessary when the expression is within the sentence and no other mark is used. Such items include persons addressed, appositives, items in addresses and dates, as well as independent phrases and clauses:

Will you help me, *Harry*, with this work?
Nan Gray, *my favorite cousin*, is here.
Tom came from Dallas, *Texas*, yesterday.
Jane was born, on June 12, 1952, in Seattle.
That boy is, *I believe*, a dependable fellow.

When an appositive (101) is an attribute or part of the proper name, or is closely connected with the word it explains, no comma is used:

Edward *the Confessor* was there.
My cousin *Nell* lives in Arizona.

501 A direct quotation equivalent to a sentence should be separated from explanatory matter by a comma or commas. But a sentence quoted within another sentence may be so closely connected with the rest of the sentence that no comma is needed:

The girl said, "Wait for me."
"Wait for me," the girl said.
"Wait," the girl said, "until I come."
Her cheerful greeting was always "How do you do today?"

No comma is used before an indirect quotation or a title in quotation marks unless there is a special need for it:

Fred said that he went to Chicago.
Longfellow wrote "The Psalm of Life."

502 Items in a date are set off by commas:

They were married on Tuesday, May 6, 1946.

In a date consisting of month and year only, commas are omitted by some writers:

In August, 1965, we were on vacation. (or August 1965)

503 Use commas for explanatory matter in connection with a direct quotation, unless stronger punctuation is necessary (495):

"It is time," she said, "for me to go home."
"It is time to go," she said; "it is very late."

504 Use commas to separate the items of a series of words, phrases, or short clauses:

The farmer sold corn, hay, oats, potatoes, and wheat.
They come from the east, from the west, from the north, and from the south.
He rose, he smiled, he began to speak.

505 A series of adjectives of the same rank modifying the same noun are separated by commas unless they are joined by conjunctions. No comma is used after the last adjective:

> We saw tall, slender, graceful trees.
> He drew the trees as tall, slender, and graceful.
> A steep and narrow path led on.

When the adjective next to the noun seems to be a part of the noun, no comma is used before it:

> He is a courteous young man. (*Courteous* modifies *young man.*)

506 A comma may sometimes be necessary for clarity of meaning:

> Ever since, Frank has been a better boy.
> You would, would you?

Quotation Marks

507 Quotation marks are used to enclose a direct quotation. They are not used with indirect quotations:

> "*You are to blame,*" she said.
> He said *that he would go home.*

508 Quotation marks or italics are used to distinguish words or letters referred to merely as words or letters. (Italics are preferred in printed form for this use.)

> You may parse the words "they" and the two "a's" in that sentence.

♦ Never use quotation marks where they are not required by the rules of composition mechanics. Do not use quotation marks for simple emphasis or for adornment.

509 Quotation marks are used with: the titles of articles; the chapter titles of books; the titles of short poems, songs, and stories; and the parts of a musical composition. (Italics are used in print for titles of books; periodicals; names of ships, airplanes, satellites, spacecraft, etc., 539.)

> He read Whittier's "Maud Muller."
> The article was called "Capturing the Imagination."
> I have read Hawthorne's "Rappaccini's Daughter."
> He listened to the "Third Movement" of the *Ninth Symphony.*

♦ One line drawn under a handwritten or typed word indicates that it would be italicized in print.

510 A long quotation of several paragraphs may have quotation marks at the beginning of each paragraph and at the end of the last paragraph. However, most long quotations are set off by additional indention or by smaller type or by both, and in this case no quotation marks are used in print. (See examples in 544, 548–550, 552, 553, 560.)

511 In reporting conversation, each speech or fragment of speech (515) no matter how short, should be in quotation marks. An uninterrupted quotation in one paragraph, though long, should have but one set of quotation marks (beginning and ending):

"Do you know me?" he asked.

"I am not sure," she replied, "that I have ever met you."

"I am your old schoolmate, Edgar Jones," he explained.

512 Nicknames and words or phrases used ironically may be put in quotations:

My friend "T-Bone" was at the picnic.

His "limousine" was a jalopy. (Be sparing of this use; it may become very annoying.)

♦ Usually quotation marks are omitted from nicknames after the first use or when the nickname (such as *Babe* Ruth) is well known. Many writers also use quotation marks to distinguish technical terms and words used in very specialized meaning.

Often it is better to avoid the use of slang and faulty diction than to apologize for it with quotation marks. Whenever the slang phrase is too expressive to admit of a more prosaic substitution, assume responsibility for using it instead of quoting it.

513 A quotation within a quotation should be enclosed in single quotation marks, and a quotation within that should be in double marks:

"I was surprised," Mary admitted, "when he said, 'I agree with Shakespeare, "All the world's a stage." ' "

514 A question mark or an exclamation mark is placed inside the quotation mark if it is a part of the quotation; outside, if it applies to the main clause. The period or the comma is always placed before the quotation mark (note example in 513); the colon or semicolon is placed outside:

"Are you ill?" she asked.

Did Father say, "Wait until tomorrow"?

Tom said, "Don't wait for me"; then he turned and walked away.

"The music was beautiful," she remarked.

If both the main clause of the sentence and the quotation are interrogative, only one question mark (529) is required:

Did Fred ask, "Where have you been?"

515 When a quotation is interrupted, an extra set of marks must be used:

"Come," he said, "as soon as you have the time."

516 There is often an erroneous impression among students that all inter-
ruptions of quotations are marked by commas. Use the sentence
marks which should be used regardless of the quotation:

"You have delayed too long already," he said. "Success comes to people
who act."

"I am sure!" she exclaimed; "there is no doubt about it."

Apostrophe

517 Use the apostrophe to indicate the omission of letters from words. It
should be placed immediately above the point of omission:

The man *isn't* here.

Do not confuse: *its* for *it's; your* for *you're; where* for *where'er.*

518 The apostrophe may be used with *s* to denote plurals of letters, figures, signs, symbols, and words considered merely as words (88):

She used two *a's,* three *b's,* two *8's* (or 8s), two *and's* (or *ands*).

519 The apostrophe is used in forming the possessive of nouns and indefinite pronouns. To form the possessive singular, add the apostrophe
and s (120):

The *bird's* plumage is brilliant.

He is *everyone's* friend.

To form the possessive plural of a noun whose plural ends in s,
add an apostrophe only (121):

Boys' suits are on sale.

♦ Some words admit of two forms (120):

Burns' or *Burns's, James'* or *James's.* (The second form seems preferred.)

520 The possessives of the personal pronouns such as *its, his, hers, ours,
yours,* and *theirs* (146) do not use the apostrophe. But indefinite pronouns, such as *either, one,* and *other,* do use the apostrophe:

The cat wants *its* (not *it's*) dinner. (*Its* is **possessive.**)

It's time to go home. (*It's* is a **contraction,** 146, 517.)

One must do *one's* duty, but always respect the *other's* rights.

521 The apostrophe is omitted from proper names in cases where a proper
noun is used as a proper adjective, a standard English usage (some
geographic names, organization or company names, etc.):

Pikes Peak, Citizens National Bank, Teachers College

Dash

522 A dash is used to mark a sudden change or break in a sentence:

The boy went there—where did he go?

"There is no—" The speaker could not go on. (No period is needed after a dash which breaks off a sentence.)

Smith told me—but don't mention this—that he was bankrupt.

523 The dash may be used to set off a parenthetic group, especially when the parenthetic expression contains commas:

His food—nuts, berries, small game—was adequate for survival.

524 The dash may be used before a summarizing statement:

He planned, he worked, he sacrificed—all these he did that he might succeed.

525 The dash may be used to lend emphasis:

For a thousand dollars—a mere thousand dollars—he betrayed his friend.

♦ A double-length dash may be used to indicate the omission of letters or words:

Have you seen Captain H——   No, but I have seen——.
lately?

Parentheses and Brackets

526 Parentheses may be used to enclose matter apart from the main thought:

If you come to see me (and I hope you do come), be sure to bring your camera.

Matter enclosed in parentheses within a sentence, even though it forms a complete declarative or imperative sentence, need not begin with a capital and need not end with a period. But if it is interrogative or exclamatory, it ends with the appropriate mark (529, 530, 531):

She says that you insulted her (did you?) and that she was furious.

527 The punctuation mark belonging to matter given before that set off by parentheses should be placed after the second parenthesis mark (see the first example sentence given in 526):

When you receive your appointment (and I hope you receive it soon), you must tell me of your plans.

When a complete, independent sentence is placed in parentheses, the final punctuation is placed inside the parentheses:

(These theories will be further explained in the next chapter.)

528 Brackets are used to enclose explanatory matter that one inserts in a quotation from another writer:

It was this poem ["The Raven"] that made Poe famous.

Question Mark

529 Place a question mark after every direct question. Although the very short declarative sentence (25) within parentheses (486) does not require a period, the short interrogative sentence (27) so used must close with a question mark (526):

>Have you seen my new hat?

>When you come to see me (why not come soon?), I will tell you about my trip to Denver.

If the main clause of a sentence and the dependent clause are both interrogative (27), only one question mark (514) is used. No question mark is used after an indirect question. After a polite request a period should be used instead of a question mark:

>Did the coach ask, "When did you return?"

>He inquired what the trouble was.

>Will you please send the check at once.

530 A question mark within parentheses is used to express uncertainty about dates or other information:

>Lucretius, 96(?)–55 B.C.

In sentences it is usually better to use *about* or *probably* than to use the question mark; in this case: Lucretius was born *about* 96 B.C.

Exclamation Mark

531 The exclamation mark is used after words, expressions, or sentences to show strong feeling or forceful utterance:

>Fire! Fire!   How terrible it was!

An exclamation within parentheses (526) retains the exclamation mark:

>She left the door unlocked (how thoughtless!) and drove to the store.

Hyphenation

532 A hyphen should be used to join words combined into a single adjective modifier: *well-to-do, self-supporting, far-flung.*

Adverbs ending in *ly* do not change into hyphened compound modifiers: a *beautifully illustrated* story.

533 The hyphen is omitted when certain compound modifiers follow the word modified and a linking verb, but true compounds retain the hyphen in this position:

>His mother is self-supporting.   His mother is well liked.

Use your dictionary as a guide to the correct usage of compounds.

534 Hyphens are used in spelling compound numbers from twenty-one to ninety-nine.

535 Fractions are hyphenated only when used as modifiers:
One half of the book is finished. (**noun**)
The box is two-thirds full. (**adverb**)
He won by a two-thirds majority. (**adjective**)

536 A compound word is one that is made up of two or more words joined together either with or without a hyphen. The purpose of a compound is to express an idea that the component parts do not express separately either in meaning or in grammatical function. They may be called *hyphemes* or *solidemes*. A purpose of the hyphen is also to avoid letter combinations that confuse the reader and to make a visual distinction for proper word stress. Examples:

1. *red coat* (garment); 2. *redcoat* (soldier); 3. *red-coated* (covered with red).

A good dictionary is the best guide to the correct form to use: two-word compound, solideme, or hypheme.

537 When it is necessary to divide a word at the end of a line, the division should be made between syllables, and a hyphen should be placed at the end of the line. Never place a hyphen at the beginning of a line. Always check the dictionary for correct syllabication of English words.

Abbreviations and Contractions

538 The following rules should be observed in using abbreviations and contractions (see also 487):

1. The use of many abbreviations in formal writing indicates carelessness on the part of the writer. However, there are a few abbreviations which are used regularly in formal writing: A.B., B.C., A.M., P.M., (when used with figures); Mr., Mrs., Ms., Dr. (when used with names).

2. It is considered impolite to abbreviate titles such as the following when used before the last name only: *captain, general, colonel, professor, president.*

3. The old rule was to place a period after each abbreviation, but there are a growing number of exceptions to the rule (see 487).

Contractions and Roman numerals used in sentences do not require periods after them:

He doesn't live here.   James II was king of England.

Periods are not used with scientific or technical symbols: H_2SO_4, sin, tan, cos.

Always refer to the dictionary for unfamiliar forms.

Italics (Underlining)

539 The following rules should be observed in using italics:

1. In writing in longhand and in typing, place one line under a word to indicate that it should be printed in italics.

2. Italicize foreign terms which have not become anglicized. The dictionary is the only safe guide in determining these words.

3. Italicize a word, phrase, or letter used as a subject of discussion (see also 508):

The word *receive* is often misspelled.

4. Use italics (see 1.) to indicate the titles of books, magazines, newspapers, and the names of ships, named trains, aircraft, and man-made spacecraft:

We have just read *The Sea Around Us* by Rachel L. Carson and an article, "Pollution of the Air," in *Harper's*.

On February 20, 1962, John H. Glenn, Jr., made three orbits of the earth in *Friendship 7*. *Apollo 15*, with astronauts Scott, Irvin, and Worden, began its famous trip to the moon on July 26, 1971.

5. In current usage, an article (285, 287) or the name of a city used in the title of a magazine or newspaper need not be italicized:

We read the Kansas City *Star* and *Natural History Magazine*.

6. It is permissible to italicize a word for emphasis, but this use of italics should be rare:

He *would* go back in spite of everything.

Numerals

540 The following rules should be observed in writing numerals:

1. Dates, street numbers, page numbers, decimals, and percents should be written in figures:

Columbus reached the New World on *October 12, 1492*.

Tom lives at 16 Spruce Street.   His address is listed on page 16.

Jim got 60 percent of the vote for class president.

2. The sign $ is not used for a sum less than one dollar:

The knife cost *sixty-five cents*.

3. The general rule for writing numbers is to spell out the number if it may be done in one or two words; otherwise, it should be written in figures:

He gave me *one thousand* dollars.

She gave me 1397 copies of the paper; there were 10,491 printed.

4. When several numbers (used as statistics) are mentioned within a short space of text use figures for all.

5. A number which represents a person's age or one denoting the hour of the day is usually spelled out:

At *three o'clock* there is to be a meeting of the students who are between *sixteen* and *eighteen* years of age.

6. Do not begin a sentence with figures:

Six hundred twenty-five (not 625) students were at the meeting.

7. It is not necessary, except in special instances such as contracts or laws, to place numerals in parentheses after written numbers; but when they are used, each should follow the number it repeats:

I am sending you *fifteen* (15) *bushels* of wheat.

8. In technical, mathematical, and business writing, figures are generally used:

125 square feet, $6.00 a pound, 4½ percent, 9.6 meters.

5

The Paragraph

Think of the house you live in as if it were a composition. Everything about your house has a specific name and function—the words of language. Each window or door, every wall or roof, is related to the whole—words in proper combination become the sentence. Each room, with its doors, windows, walls, ceiling, and furniture, becomes a unit of the whole—the sentences in logical sequence become the paragraph. Your house is made up of a series of rooms (unless it is a one-room house!)—the paragraphs in their turn become a composition. Compositions, like the houses people live in, have many styles: essay, story, letter, news report, speech, research paper, sermon, poem, novel, play, review, précis.

Structure and Analysis

541 WHAT IS A PARAGRAPH?   The paragraph is usually described as a group of sentences developing a single topic. Sometimes a paragraph may consist of a single topic sentence; at other times, several paragraphs may be needed to develop a topic.

542 LENGTH OF THE PARAGRAPH   The length of the paragraph in general writing is determined primarily by the extent to which the ideas are developed. This rule, however, is not arbitrary and may be modified, as for instance in the business letter (589-11), in which the short paragraph is more effective than the longer one. In dialogue, of course, each speech is separately paragraphed as a rule.

543 PARAGRAPH SENSE Every good writer develops a paragraph sense, just as he develops a sentence sense (36). This sense may be acquired by thinking in terms of topics and by adhering strictly to each topic under discussion.

544 TOPIC SENTENCE The sentence that presents the topic to be discussed is called the **topic sentence**. It is often stated at the beginning of the paragraph—but it may occur at any point in a paragraph—and its position may be varied to avoid monotony. The paragraph following, from Emerson's "Compensation," illustrates the beginning topic sentence:

> *A man cannot speak but he judges himself.* With his will or against his will he draws his portrait to the eye of his companions by every word. Every opinion reacts on him who utters it. It is a threadball thrown at a mark, but the other end remains in the thrower's bag. Or rather, it is a harpoon thrown at the whale, unwinding, as it flies, a coil of cord in the boat, and, if the harpoon is not good, or not well thrown, it will go nigh to cut the steersman in twain or to sink the boat.

♦ Often no one sentence expresses the topic. But make sure that, except for transition paragraphs, a topic can be identified for each paragraph.

545 DEVELOPING THE TOPIC There are many ways of developing the topic, some of the most common being the use of *details, examples, comparison* or *contrast, cause and effect,* or a combination of any two or more of these methods. An illustration is given for each of the first three:

1. **Details.** Giving details makes a topic more vivid and develops at greater length what is suggested in the topic. Here is a familiar paragraph from "The Legend of Sleepy Hollow," by Washington Irving.

> All was now bustle and hubbub in the late quiet schoolroom. The scholars were hurried through their lessons, without stopping at trifles; those who were nimble skipped over half with impunity, and those who were tardy had a smart application now and then in the rear, to quicken their speed, or help them over a tall word. Books were flung aside without being put away on the shelves, inkstands were overturned, benches thrown down, and the whole school was turned loose an hour before the usual time, bursting forth like a legion of young imps, yelping and racketing about the green, in joy of their early emancipation.

2. **Examples.** Concrete examples are given to illustrate the general suggestion of the topic:

Riverside Park is noted for the beauty and variety of its native trees. Along the river to the south are many excellent specimens of elm, sycamore, cottonwood, and hackberry. To the west, covering several acres, is a grove of tall, beautiful black walnut trees, shading here and there a less stately mulberry. To the north the park abounds in large shapely oaks, some of which thrust out protecting arms above clumps of timid redbuds. Other less prominent specimens scattered throughout the park are ash, box elder, and Osage orange.

3. **Contrast.** Through contrast, differences are made to stand out more prominently. Notice the effect of this method in the paragraph below, from "The Country Church," by Washington Irving:

As I have brought these families into contrast, I must notice their behavior in church. That of the nobleman's family was quiet, serious, and attentive. Not that they appeared to have any fervor of devotion, but rather a respect for sacred things, and sacred places, inseparable from good breeding. The others, on the contrary, were in a perpetual flutter and whisper; they betrayed a continual consciousness of finery, and the sorry ambition of being the wonders of a rural congregation.

In developing a topic explaining a process, such as building something, follow its normal order. The construction of an article would be described by the selection of the materials on through the different stages in a step-by-step sequence.

546 Mechanics of Writing Paragraphs

1. Indent the first line of each paragraph. In longhand, it is customary to indent about an inch; in typing, the usual indentation is five or ten spaces.

2. Do not leave a part of a line blank except at the close of the paragraph.

3. Except when the length of the paragraph is arbitrary, as it is in dialogue, it should seldom be made either extremely long or short.

4. In dialogue, begin a paragraph with each change of speaker.

5. Keep the left margin of the paragraph uniform and the right margin reasonably so. Paragraph indention should be uniform.

6. Make the transition from paragraph to paragraph easy and natural, sometimes by the use of appropriate transition words (549), but always by proper arrangement.

♦ Some business firms do not indent typewritten paragraphs in their letters. This style is called **flush-paragraphing** or **block style.** Sometimes, too, printers begin paragraphs at the margin as an element of the typographic design.

Paragraph Requirements

547 The paragraph, like the sentence (433–435), must have **unity, coherence, and emphasis.**

548 **Unity in the paragraph** is attained when every sentence bears directly upon the topic of that particular paragraph. Any departure from the central topic means that a new paragraph should be formed. In the following paragraph the italicized sentence is irrelevant and therefore should be eliminated:

> You will find in this car all the qualities you desire most in a motor car—economy, style, comfort, efficiency, endurance. With its low first cost and inexpensive operation it has long been the acknowledged economy leader. It is also a style leader, and it offers every modern comfort expected in even the most expensive type of car. *Owners are enthusiastic about it because of its easy steering.* In speed and safety and sureness of high performance it defies competition. Year after year it continues to give superior service unhampered by the inconvenience and expense of repair.

549 **Coherence in the paragraph** results from the correct arrangement of the parts of a paragraph—an arrangement in which each part of the paragraph is often aided by the use of appropriate transitional words, but too many such words results in a heavy, stilted style. Careful arrangement is the important means of attaining coherence. Transition words are so numerous that one may be found to suit the exact need of almost any transition.

Transition words are used to show: (a) passing of time; (b) addition; (c) contrast or opposition; (d) comparison and similarity; (e) concession, admission of facts; (f) sequence or numerical order; (g) result; (h) summary.

Some of the more commonly used of these words and phrases are *furthermore, however, for this reason, consequently, in addition, notwithstanding, all things considered, to this end, hence, above all, for example, as a consequence, on the contrary, nevertheless, as a result, but, otherwise, yet, still, meanwhile, presently, finally, in conclusion, for instance, therefore,* and *accordingly.*

The paragraph below illustrates the smooth use of transition words. In order to see the importance of arrangement, try placing the next to the last sentence as the concluding sentence. This will show the loss in force of the paragraph that is not coherent:

> You may be sure that I am pleased with the adjustment you have made about the returned goods. This adjustment is in keeping with the fine spirit of honesty and fairness that you have continually

shown me in the years in which I have been doing business with you. As a consequence of your excellent treatment, I have continued to give you the bulk of my orders. In addition, I have used my influence to turn other business to you. As in the past, I shall continue to show you my appreciation in this practical way.

550 **Emphasis in the paragraph** results from giving stress to the important ideas. If more space is given to the important ideas than to the unimportant, there is possibility of interfering with unity and coherence; therefore it may be best to give emphasis by position. The beginning or the close of the paragraph is the most emphatic position. The paragraph below from "The Masque of the Red Death," a short story by Poe, is a good illustration of proper emphasis in the paragraph. Note how by position the emphasis is given by *Red Death*. It is obvious that a shifting of the last sentence to the middle of the paragraph would weaken the entire effect:

> And now was acknowledged the presence of the Red Death. He had come like a thief in the night. And one by one dropped the revelers in the blood-bedewed halls of their revel, and each died in the despairing posture of his fall. And the life of the ebony clock went out with that of the last of the gay. And the flames of the tripods expired. And Darkness and Decay and the Red Death held illimitable dominion over all.

Forms of Discourse

551 There are four types of expression known as **forms of discourse,** and every paragraph illustrates one of these types or a combination of two or more of them. These four forms are **exposition, description, narration, argumentation.**

Exposition

552 Exposition is explaining, and it is the form most frequently used. It is, however, often closely associated with the other forms, particularly with description. In fact, exposition and description are so closely blended sometimes that it is difficult to distinguish between them. Exposition depends for its effectiveness on the use of accurate, concrete words instead of vague, abstract terms. The paragraph below illustrates clear exposition in very simple, accurate terms:

> When you speak, your vocal chords vibrate. The vibrations cause changes in the pressure of the air. Waves of sound are set up. When the sound waves reach another person, they strike the eardrum. The eardrum vibrates according to the changing pressure of the air on it. The person hears.

Description

553 Description is picturing in words. As has been pointed out (552), it is closely associated with the other forms, particularly exposition, with which it is often almost inseparably blended. Pure description is seldom met with in discourse, for it needs the other forms to give it movement. It is made vivid by the use of meaningful words, particularly adjectives (275) and nouns (39). The paragraph given below, from Irving's "Rural Life in England," is a good illustration of description. Note the descriptive words *imposing, vast, vivid, gigantic, rich, solemn, woodland, silent, natural, glassy, sequestered, quivering, yellow, sleeping, limpid, rustic, sylvan, green, dank, classic:*

> Nothing can be more imposing than the magnificence of English park scenery. Vast lawns that extend like sheets of vivid green, with here and there clumps of gigantic trees, heaping up rich piles of foliage: the solemn pomp of groves and woodland glades, with the deer trooping in silent herds across them; the hare bounding away to the covert; or the pheasant, suddenly bursting upon the wing; the brook, taught to wind in natural meanderings or expand into a glassy lake; the sequestered pool, reflecting the quivering trees, with the yellow leaf sleeping on its bosom, and the trout roaming fearlessly about its limpid waters; while some rustic temple of sylvan statue, grown green and dank with age, gives an air of classic sanctity to the seclusion.

Narration

554 Narration is a rehearsal of events which may have been either real or imaginary; it is the telling of a story, whether the story is truth or fiction. This may be done best by the selection of events that are essential to the story, by the proper use of transitional expressions that show: (a) continuation of thought; (b) passing of time; (c) result; (d) opposition. It is usually associated with exposition and description, and it must give the effect of movement from event to event. The many stories with which we are familiar are examples of narration. Those who write or tell stories should observe these precautions for successful narration: **Make a prompt, effective beginning; stick to** the story; **tell the story simply; end it promptly.**

Point of view is another element that is of key importance in narration. First-person point of view (*I*) and third-person point of view (*he, she, they*) indicate either that the teller is an actor in the story or that the teller is an observer of a story about others. Consistency in the use of verb tenses and transitional words is essential since they differ for the two points of view.

Argumentation

555 **Argumentation** is an effort to show by logical arrangement of facts that a statement is true or false, as in a mathematical demonstration such as the proof of a proposition in geometry. When one attempts to establish a new conviction in written matter, one explains facts favorable to that conviction: this is argumentation. To be successful in argumentation, one must exercise the same tact and skills as in the other forms. Much good may be achieved through written argumentation, but in the verbal contacts of everyday life, tact must be applied.

Development of Creative Expression

556 **Creative expression** is the communication of a feeling or experience that is worth sharing with others just for its own sake. This is the type of expression which at its best gives us our literature. But all of us, whether or not we have the urge or the genius to become great creative artists, should give thought to creative expression, since it may help us to observe more closely the things about us. We become more critical of ourselves and others and thus better able to analyze our own behavior and to be more sympathetic with the behavior of others. Through this type of expression we may eventually have a broader understanding of life and its problems.

Précis-Writing

557 **ABILITY TO CONDENSE EXPRESSION** It is important that one develop the ability to express one's thoughts in well-organized paragraphs of the different forms of discourse (551), and it is of no less importance that one should learn how to condense one's meaning into the fewest possible words. The ability to condense the expression of others to the fewest possible words should also be acquired. Such a condensed form of expression retains the thought and emphasis of the original and is called a **précis**.

558 **THE PRÉCIS** A standard definition of the précis is a "brief summary of essential points, statements, or facts." It differs from a **paraphrase** in that it is much shorter and more precisely and accurately written. It must retain in few words the ideas of the original, and these ideas must be clearly and forcefully expressed. The length of the précis may vary with the intensity of the thought, but a good general average would be to reduce the number of words to one third or one fourth the original. The writer of the précis must grasp the entire meaning of the expression to be condensed (562).

559 SUGGESTIONS FOR PRÉCIS–WRITING Précis-writing is excellent exercise for inexperienced writers who have a tendency to wordiness (462). Here are some general suggestions:

1. Be sure you understand what you are trying to condense.
2. Follow the original without changing the order of the thought.
3. Use your own words.
4. Write as clearly and forcefully as possible.

560 ILLUSTRATION Below is an illustration of précis-writing in which each of five summaries of a paragraph is rated by expert authority. The test paragraph, given first, is followed by instructions for grading and five summaries. (The extract is "Selection V, Form A" from the *Poley Précis Test*, a standard test by Irwin C. Poley, Public School Publishing Company, Bloomington, Illinois. Reprinted by permission of the publisher.)

> Vandalism in the parks is all too typical of one side of the American character. We seem incapable of bearing in mind an idea of decency in the abstract. As guests, if our host is a friend, we treat him with courtesy; but if he is unknown and not at hand to watch us we concede him no rights whatever; as hunters borrowing somebody's land we drop cigarettes and start forest fires; as campers borrowing somebody's woods we have a litter of cans and refuse that is notorious. . . . We are callous to the idea that things ought not to be destroyed, no matter who owns them or who will use them. . . . Park vandals are guests of the public, and they should have enough regard for the host not to destroy his property. They use the parks in common with many other people and they should have a thought to the comfort of others.
>
> Editorial, New York *World.*

INSTRUCTIONS: Below are five summaries of the paragraph just given. Try to rate the summaries as to accuracy and completeness. The ratings as given by the author of the test appear after the last summary.

    a. Americans are apt to be discourteous in their treatment of public parks. They should remember that consideration is due as much to an absent or public host as to a present or private one.

    b. In America the parks are littered with trash, especially cigarettes, which may start a forest fire. Private property should be respected as much as public.

    c. Private property should be respected as much as public property, if not more. Parks are sure to be littered with refuse, and public camping sites are spoiled.

   d. If hunters borrow land, they should be careful not to drop
   cigarettes and thus start a fire. Campers should not leave a
   litter of refuse behind them; even if they do not know the
   owner, they should be considerate of the property.

   e. Americans should learn to get along pleasantly with people
   they meet in the park. The public is our host, and individuals
   should try to act as courteously to one another as they do in
   Europe.

The five summaries are rated as follows: *a* best expresses the thought
of the original paragraph; *b*, *c*, and *e* are inaccurate (that is, they
contain actual errors of statement); *d* is inadequate (that is, it misses
the central thought of the original paragraph although it contains no
error of statement).

Critical Reading

561 READING "There is an art of reading, as well as an art of thinking, and
an art of writing." This aphorism by Isaac D'Israeli, written in 1791,
is still as valid as when it was written. Critical reading has the major
task of grasping the thought of the writer; a secondary task is observing
the mechanical techniques used in expressing it. These techniques include the spelling, grammar, punctuation, and capitalization employed
in writing down the thoughts. A reading of this kind is referred to as
proofreading.

562 READING FOR THOUGHT Reading for content may be done for a
number of reasons. One may read the newspapers as a daily habit for
the current events reported there. Or one may read magazines and
books from a desire to learn about the opinions and experiences of
others or to enlarge personal horizons.

A more serious purpose of the reader may be to gather material for
a paper or a speech through extensive reading in a library. The latter
type of reading is usually accompanied with note-taking, the purpose
of which is to gather facts.

Every reader should learn to grasp and quickly pinpoint the main
ideas while reading. The principal facts in a newspaper article may
be learned by reading the headlines and lead paragraphs. One should
train oneself to glean from every paragraph the necessary facts by
writing brief, clear notes or a précis (557). Accurate reading and
expert précis-writing go hand in hand, both being invaluable aids to
anyone who wishes to attain effective expression.

563 PROOFREADING In addition to learning to get the thought from written expression, one must learn to detect mechanical errors in it.
Reading for the purpose of correcting mechanical errors is called
proofreading, though in the strictest sense this term is applied only

to the correction of proof sheets for a printer. You may use any simple system of marking errors in proofreading your own work or the work of others. Appropriate rules for correcting such errors are to be found in the various sections of this book. Those interested in reading real printer's proof will find a list of standard symbols in *Webster's New Collegiate Dictionary*, page 922.

Writing Verse

564 EXPRESSION IN VERSE   Verse is a form of composition which is very different from prose. It is so constructed that it has rhythm—rhythm is heard by the ear and not seen by the eye—and this rhythm is generally produced by a regular arrangement of stressed and unstressed syllables.

The writing of verse is a satisfying creative expression and good practice in acquiring skill in the use of words. In addition, the writing of light or humorous verse may be entertaining. It gives variety to expression that, in prose, has a tendency to become sedate. The next few sections explain the structure of verse.

565 VERSE FORMS   Before one attempts to write verse, one should become familiar with the simple mechanics of versification given here.

1. **Verse.** The term *verse* may be applied (by a figure of speech called *synedoche*, the substitution of the name of a part for the whole, 682) to rhythmical composition in general, but in a more restricted sense it indicates a line of verse. A verse, then, of poetry is one line, not a group of lines.

2. **Stanza.** A stanza is a group of lines (verses) bound together by some rhyme scheme (570) which is usually repeated in the poem.

3. **Foot.** A foot is simply a unit of measurement of the rhythm of a verse and consists of accented and unaccented syllables.

4. **Kinds of Feet.** There are four kinds of feet in popular use, though there are others less often used. The four are iambic, trochaic, anapaestic, and dactylic.

   a. **Iambic.** The iambic foot consists of one *unaccented* syllable followed by one *accented*: ex-PEL.

   b. **Trochaic.** A trochaic foot is made up of one *accented* syllable followed by one *unaccented*: BEAU-ty.

   c. **Anapaestic.** An anapaestic foot has two *unaccented* syllables followed by one *accented*: in-ter-VENE.

   d. **Dactylic.** A dactylic foot has one *accented* syllable followed by two *unaccented*: BEAU-ti-ful.

5. **Number of Feet in a Line.** A line (verse) is classified by the number of feet it contains. A line of one foot is called a **monometer;** two feet, **dimeter;** three feet, **trimeter;** four feet, **tetrameter;** five feet, **pentameter;** six feet, **hexameter;** seven feet, **heptameter;** and eight feet, **octameter.**

566 **THE NAME OF THE LINE**   A line gets its name from the number and kind of feet it contains. For example, a line of five iambic feet is called **iambic pentameter.** Here are illustrations taken from familiar poems:

(iambic tetrameter) I thínk | that Í | shall nev́- | er seé. ("Trees")

(trochaic tetrameter) Téll me | nót in | móurn-ful | núm-bers.
                                                                  ("A Psalm of Life")

(anapaestic tetrameter) For the moón | nev-er beáms | with-out bríng- | ing me dreáms.   ("Annabel Lee")

(dactylic hexameter) Bláck were her | eýes as the | bér-ry that | gró͟ws on the | thórn by the | wáy-side.   ("Evangeline")

567 **RHYME**   Rhyme is correspondence, in two or more words, of ending sounds beginning with the last accented vowel. The preceding consonant sounds should be different, though rhymes are not always perfect:

Rhymes: relate, sedate; willing, fulfilling

Imperfect rhymes: relate, elate; imply, reply

568 **RHYTHM**   Verse rhythm is the regular recurrence of accented and unaccented syllables. Rhythm is necessary to verse, but the use of rhyme is not. Verse with regular rhythm but without rhyme is called blank verse. Another kind of verse without rhyme is called free verse. It has rhythmical cadence, but does not depend on a strict arrangement of the accented and unaccented syllables.

569 **BLANK VERSE**   Any unrhymed verse may be called blank verse, but this term is applied especially to iambic pentameter, the kind of verse used in Shakespeare's plays.

570 **RHYME SCHEME**   A stanza usually has a regular rhyme scheme. That is, each stanza in a given poem has corresponding lines which rhyme with each other. Rhyme scheme is represented by letters of the alphabet; a first rhyme is represented by *a*, a second by *b*, and so on.

571 **STANZA FORMS**   Some of the stanza forms much used are the **sonnet** (572–574), the **limerick** (576), and the **quatrain.** The example of the quatrain given below is from MacLeish's "You, Andrew Marvel." It is made up of four iambic tetrameter lines (566) rhyming alternately (*a, b, a, b*):

        And here face down beneath the sun
        And here upon earth's noonward height
        To feel the always coming on
        The always rising of the night:

572 SONNET   The sonnet is a form which has long been popular. It consists of fourteen iambic pentameter lines with a strict rhyme scheme. There are two well-known forms, the **Italian** or **Petrarchan** sonnet, and the **English** or **Shakespearean** sonnet.

573 ITALIAN SONNET   The Italian sonnet has the more rigid rhyme scheme, which demands but two rhymes in the first eight lines (octave) and restricts the rhyming of the last six lines (sestet). The rhyme of the octave is *a b b a a b b a*. The sestet may vary its rhyme scheme, though the last two lines should not rhyme together.

    As an example of the Italian sonnet, here is one of the best known —that by Keats in· which he confused the Spanish conqueror of Mexico, Cortés, with·Balboa, a Spanish explorer in Panama:

ON FIRST LOOKING INTO CHAPMAN'S HOMER

Much have | I trav | eled in | the realms | of gold,	*a*
And many goodly states and kingdoms seen;	*b*
Round many western islands have I been	*b*
Which bards in fealty of Apollo hold.	*a*
Oft of one wide expanse had I been told	*a*
That deep-brow'd Homer ruled as his demesne;	*b*
Yet did I never breathe its pure serene	*b*
Till I heard Chapman speak out loud and bold:	*a*
Then felt I like some watcher of the skies	*c*
When a new planet swims into his ken;	*d*
Or like stout Cortez when with eagle eyes	*c*
He stared at the Pacific—and all his men	*d*
Looked at each other with a wild surmise—	*c*
Silent, upon a peak in Darien.	*d*

574 ENGLISH SONNET   The English or Shakespearean sonnet is made up of three quatrains with alternate rhyme and a rhyming couplet. The rhyme scheme used by Shakespeare is *a b a b/c d c d/e f e f/g g*. One of Shakespeare's sonnets is given here:

SONNET LXIV

When I | have seen | by Time's | fell hand | defaced	*a*
The rich proud cost of outworn buried age;	*b*
When sometime lofty towers I see down-razed	*a*
And brass eternal slave to mortal rage;	*b*
When I have seen the hungry ocean gain	*c*
Advantage on the kingdom of the shore,	*d*

And the firm soil win of the watery main,   c
Increasing store with loss and loss with store;   d
When I have seen such interchange of state,   e
Or state itself confounded in decay;   f
Ruin hath taught me thus to ruminate,   e
That Time will come and take my love away.   f
This thought is as a death, which cannot choose   g
But weep to have that which it fears to lose.   g

575 TYPES OF VERSE   There are many types of verse ranging from nonsense rhymes to the most exalted poetry. Only the types of verse
expressing emotion as well as idea should be called poetry. The
limerick below is a good example of light verse; the two sonnets (573,
574) are classed as poetry.

576 LIGHT VERSE   Light or humorous verse may be written on a variety of
subjects or in imitation of familiar poems or songs. A bit of writing in
imitation of another is called a **parody**. The example of light verse
below is in limerick form. The first, second, and fifth rhyming lines
of the limerick are roughly anapaestic trimeter (565). The third and
fourth lines are anapaestic dimeter rhyming together. Any line of a
limerick may begin with either one or two unaccented syllables as
does this one by Edward Lear:

There was an old man with a beard
Who said, "It is just as I feared!
    Two Owls and a Hen,
    Four Larks and a Wren,
Have all built their nests in my beard."

6

The Whole Composition

> I keep six honest serving men
> (They taught me all I know);
> Their names are *What* and *Why* and *When*
> And *How* and *Where* and *Who*.
>
> RUDYARD KIPLING, *Just So Stories* (1902)

Planning the Composition

577 THE COMPOSITION AS A UNIT It is necessary that not only the sentences and paragraphs each maintain unity, coherence, and emphasis but also that the composition as a whole maintain these three qualities. The composition must be a unit with its parts so arranged as to show clearly their relationship. In addition, the most important ideas must be in those positions that give them the greatest emphasis—the beginning and the close.

578 ORGANIZING MATERIAL A very simple plan for news stories may be made by answering the questions: *Who? When? Where? What? Why?*

Who—Our club
When—Next Thursday
Where—Glenwood Park
What—A picnic
Why—To entertain our new members

Another excellent general plan for organizing material for a composition is to jot down all thoughts on the subject as they occur, at first with no attempt at orderly arrangement, and then later to assemble the ideas in related groups as a complete outline. The topics in such an outline should be arranged in their logical order, somewhat as they are arranged in the outline below:

MARKET GARDENING

1. *Deciding* what to plant
2. *Selecting* the seed
3. *Preparing* the soil
4. *Planting* the seed
5. *Cultivating* the growing plants
6. *Gathering* the produce
7. *Preparing* the produce for market
8. *Selling* the produce

579 TOPIC OUTLINE A topic outline is made up of headings which indicate the main ideas for the composition. Terms of the same rank should be parallel. For example, the main headings in the outline below are all nouns: Pleasure, Health, Citizenship:

I. Pleasure
    A. Relaxation from study
    B. Enjoyment of competition
II. Health
    A. Stimulation of bodily functions
    B. Increase in mental alertness
III. Citizenship
    A. Development of cooperation
    B. Development of regard for others

580 SENTENCE OUTLINES The sentence outline has complete sentences:

TENNIS IS A GOOD GAME FOR STUDENTS

I. It provides pleasure.
    A. The change from study to play relieves tension.
    B. The thrill of competition is stimulating.
II. It promotes health.
    A. The outdoor exercise is good for the body.
    B. The keen interest in the game keeps the brain alert.
III. It develops good citizenship.
    A. The contact with others discourages selfishness.
    B. The rules of the game make necessary a regard for the rights of others.

♦ The **paragraph outline** is made by expanding the material into complete paragraphs. It is not so frequently used as are the two forms given—topic and sentence.

581 NUMBERING THE ELABORATE OUTLINE The subscripts are properly labeled this way: I., A., 1., 2., 3. . . . , a., b., c. . . . , (1), (2), (3), . . . , (a), (b), (c), . . . ; I., B., 1., . . . , a., . . . , (1) . . . , (a) . . . ; II., A., 1., . . . , a., . . . , (1), . . . , (a), . . . ; II., B., ... 1. etc.

Written Composition

582 There are two general classes of composition—oral and written. Written composition will be discussed first.

583 **Written composition** includes every form of writing. This brief outline may give some idea of its great variety and importance.

584 TYPES OF WRITTEN COMPOSITION Of the many types of written composition the following are some of the most familiar: fiction, history, biography, essay, poetry, newspaper reporting, and the letter. Because the letter is the type of composition most widely used by people in general, it is discussed in detail.

585 LETTERS Comparatively few people become professional writers, but everyone has occasion to write letters. The successful businessperson must write letters of professional quality, and everyone must at times write letters of personal importance.

586 CLASSES OF LETTERS There are only two general classes of letters—business and social. The business letter includes all forms written for business purposes. The social letter varies from the informal letter of friendship to the most formal note. A letter, of course, may be a combination of the two classes.

Business Correspondence

587 BUSINESS LETTERS The writing of business letters is not confined to those who are in business. Practically every person has occasion to write about transactions not related to the social affairs of life.

588 IMPORTANCE OF THE BUSINESS LETTER A great part of the world's business is transacted through exchange of letters; therefore the business letter is of tremendous importance. The very difficult art of business-letter writing is challenging the finest talent in the world of commerce today.

589 REQUIREMENTS OF A GOOD BUSINESS LETTER Requirements of a good business letter are the following: promptness, accuracy, clearness,

economy, completeness, correctness, courtesy, neatness, friendliness, effective sentence construction, proper paragraphing, proper diction and correct spelling, and freedom from hackneyed expressions. Each of these is worthy of short comment:

1. **Promptness.** A business letter should be answered at once.

2. **Accuracy.** A letter that is not accurate in form or in content implies that the writer is either careless or lacking in ability to communicate.

3. **Clearness.** One of the first essentials of a business letter is clearness. Weak sentences (437-449) may cause confusion of meaning.

4. **Economy.** A letter should be so written that every word serves a distinct purpose. It should be as brief as is consistent with clearness and courtesy but all sentences should be complete.

5. **Completeness.** A business letter should be so complete in itself as to make unnecessary any further correspondence to supplement it.

6. **Correctness.** No letter can be strong enough in other ways to overcome the handicap of incorrect language or form.

7. **Courtesy.** A letter lacking in courtesy reflects discredit on the writer and on the business he represents. An effective means of showing courtesy is by stressing the *you* rather than the *I*.

8. **Neatness.** Neatness depends on the paper, margins, spacing, and typing. The paper is usually 8½ by 11 inches and of a good quality of white with envelopes to match. (Business letters should never be written on stationery meant for social letters.) Margins should be so spaced that they are in correct proportion to the letter, and the typed space should appear as a picture correctly set in a frame. Usually single spacing is used except between paragraphs and parts of the letter, where spacing is double. The typing should be clear and free from untidy, obvious erasures.

9. **Friendliness.** Effective business letters are those which have a friendly tone.

10. **Effective Sentence Construction.** Make all sentences effective (433-436). See that they are free from weaknesses (438-448) and that they are varied (421-431).

11. **Proper Paragraphing.** The correct paragraphing of a business letter aids much in making its meaning clear. Long paragraphs are not so clear as shorter ones. Most writers of business letters prefer paragraphs of not more than six or eight lines. Proper arrangement of paragraphs is also vital.

12. **Proper Diction and Correct Spelling.** Each word should be chosen to convey the exact meaning intended, and no word should ever be misspelled.

13. **Freedom from Hackneyed Expressions.** There are expressions in business correspondence which have become obsolete through overuse. No modern streamlined letter should be marred by even one of these relics. The following are a few of those that were once most frequently used: *and oblige, as per, at hand, beg to state, early date, enclosed herewith,*

esteemed favor, has come to hand, kind favor, please note, recent date, we thank you kindly, we would advise, your favor of, yours to hand.

590 **PARTS OF THE BUSINESS LETTER** There are six main parts of a business letter: heading, inside address, salutation, body, complimentary close, signature. Other parts of the business letter which might be included are the initials placed at the left lower margin of a dictated letter to indicate the dictator and the stenographer, or typist, and the outside address (on the envelope). Each of these parts require separate discussion.

591 **HEADING OF THE BUSINESS LETTER** The heading is placed at the upper right-hand corner (of stationery that does not have a printed letterhead) and consists of the exact address of the writer and the date. Its length will determine the number of lines it requires, though it usually consists of three or four lines. The first line should give the smallest division, such as box number, name of building, or street and number; then comes the name of the city and the state, followed by the Zip Code number. The last line is the date.

A date that is stated in terms of the day, month, and year is correct in form but this form is not as yet as widely used in letter-writing as it is in record-keeping: 15 December 1972 (15 Dec 72).

You may abbreviate the name of the state but not the city, and write the street number in figures. Today's writers do not abbreviate the name of the month in headings. Of course, where printed stationery is used, the letterhead includes all the heading except the date. The day of the month and the year are usually written in figures.

592 **FORM OF THE HEADING** The heading may be either of the block type or the indented. In the block type each line begins exactly the same distance from the right and left margins; in the indented type each succeeding line is spaced uniformly to the right. Examples are given below. The block form is almost always used in typing; the indented form may be used when writing in longhand:

```
1255 Walnut Street          1255 Walnut Street
Denver, Colorado  80202       Denver, Colorado  80202
December 15, 19--               December 15, 19--
```

593 **PUNCTUATION OF THE HEADING** Almost no punctuation appears in the heading except for the comma between the names of the city and state and the comma between the numbers indicating the day and year in the date.

594 **INSIDE ADDRESS** The inside address should be placed at the left margin below the heading; and it should give the proper courtesy title and business title, if any, correct name, and complete address of the person for whom the letter is intended. The form should be the same as that of the heading.

```
Mr. Hugh J. Dunn
4230 Main Street
Houston, Texas   77002
```

595 **SALUTATION** The salutation is placed at the left margin two spaces below the inside address. The following are appropriate salutations in greeting an individual whose name is known: *Dear Mr.* _____, *Dear Mrs.* _____, *Dear Ms.* _____, *Dear Miss* _____. In letters addressed to a firm or to an individual whose name is not known, *Dear Sir or Madam* is the most common greeting.

There are special forms of address and salutation for high dignitaries of the Church and the State and courtesy demands that they be followed exactly. *Webster's New Collegiate Dictionary*, under "Forms of Address," page 1528, gives a list of such forms.

596 **CAPITALIZATION OF THE SALUTATION** If the salutation consists of but two words, both are capitalized; but in a salutation such as *My dear General Smith*, the *dear* is not capitalized.

597 **PUNCTUATION OF THE SALUTATION** The punctuation mark used after the salutation in a business letter is the colon (494). There is a present trend to add friendliness to the business letter; therefore the comma, less formal than the colon, might be used after the salutation of the more informal business letter to a friend.

598 **BODY** The body of the letter is the message. It should conform to all rules of good writing (see 589). The sentences should be made effective (see 421–463). The paragraphs should be short and forceful (see 547–550). All words should be well chosen, and each should add something to the effectiveness of the letter. Be careful to avoid the worn-out expressions (see 589–613) that brand a letter as stilted. Make your letter a part of you—give it your personality.

The opening sentence is especially vital, for on its effectiveness may depend the fate of the entire message. The first sentence should be specific and it should make some personal appeal to the reader. It should stress *you*, not *I*. It should never begin with any of the following meaningless references to the receipt of a letter: *Pursuant to your request of the fifth, Answering your letter of October 5, We beg to acknowledge receipt of your letter of June 4, We are in receipt of your letter of May 9, Your letter of recent date at hand, Acknowledging yours of recent date, Supplementing your letter of March 16, We have your letter of April 3, Replying to yours of August 12, Complying with your request of recent date, Referring to your favor of June 6.* Such expressions were once acceptable but they are now in the scrap heap of clichés except in certain legal correspondence.

The closing sentence is also very important. It should leave the reader feeling that he or she has just made contact with a cordial, friendly person.

When a letter is more than a page in length, the name of the person addressed, the page number, and the date should be placed at the top of each additional page. The margins should be the same for all pages. Five lines or more should appear on the last page.

599 COMPLIMENTARY CLOSE   The complimentary close should be consistent with the other parts of the letter. It should never be preceded by the participial expressions once so popular, such as *Thanking you for your favor, Hoping this will be satisfactory, Awaiting your reply.* The last sentence should be complete, and it should say something vital. The close needs no such out-dated expressions as *I am* or *I remain* as an introduction. End the message with a forceful, appropriate sentence; then begin the close about the center of the page below. The following are correct in business letters: *Yours truly, Very truly yours, Yours sincerely, Sincerely yours.* The first word only of the close is capitalized. The close is punctuated with a comma at the end.

600 SIGNATURE   The signature is placed just below the close. Place the signature so that its first letter is below the first letter of the close. Usually the writer's name is also typed just beneath the longhand signature or with the initials of the typist at the left. Every letter should, of course, be signed in ink. The signature of a letter sent out by a business organization may include the name and position of the writer. The following are examples:

Sincerely,

Frances Wilson

Frances Wilson
Sales Manager

RHN: Frances Wilson

In signing a business letter, a married woman or a widow uses her own name, such as *Ann Clarke Brown*, not her married social name, *Mrs. Frank R. Brown*. She may write *Mrs.* in parentheses before the name or she may write her married name in parentheses below the signature:

(*style 1*)

(Mrs.) Louise C. Randall

(*style 2*)

Louise C. Randall
(Mrs. Robert J. Randall)

A divorced woman may choose to use her unmarried or married surname, alone or with any title:

Janice A. Jordan
(Miss) Janice A. Jordan
(Mrs.) Janice A. Jordan Taylor

In a dictated letter initials are typed at the lower left margin to identify the dictator and the stenographer. If there is an enclosure, it is indicated just under the initials; if more than one by ( ):

```
FBJ:RHM          FBJ/rhm          FBJ-RHM
Encl.            Encl.            Enc. (3)
```

601 FOLDING THE LETTER   The business letter is generally written on one side of a sheet of paper of commercial size, 8½ by 11 inches. When this is to be enclosed in an envelope of the larger size (usually No. 10 —4⅛ by 9½ inches), fold up from the bottom about one third and down from the top slightly less. Place it in the envelope with the free edge at the top and toward the gummed flap (away from you). If the envelope to be used is of the smaller size (usually No. 6¾— 3⅝ by 6½ inches), fold the lower part of the sheet over the upper so that the horizontal crease is slightly below the center; then fold the right-hand part so that the vertical crease is about one third from the right; then fold from the left so that the second vertical crease is slightly less than one third the width of the sheet from the left. Place this in the envelope with the free edge at the top and away from the gummed flap of the envelope (toward you). Be sure that all folds are straight and that all edges are even. The good effect of a letter may be lessened by careless or slovenly folding.

602 OUTSIDE ADDRESS The outside address, or address on the envelope, should be the same in content as the inside address. The first line gives the name and the title of the person addressed, the second line gives the street number, and the third line gives the name of the city, the state, and the Zip Code number. The first line should be about the center of the envelope from top to bottom, though some writers prefer that it be slightly below. The name should be correctly spelled (a misspelled name is unforgivable!), and it should be written exactly as the one addressed is known to use it. If a business title is long, it should be placed on a separate line. Abbreviations are optional, but some careful writers avoid them, preferring to write out such words as the names of states, streets, and avenues. An address is usually single-spaced. Special directions, such as General Delivery and Personal, are placed in the lower left corner. The writer's name and address should be in the upper left corner. The following illustration is correct:

```
H. L. Wilson
2145 Valleyroad Avenue South
Springfield, Missouri  65804




                 Mr. Frank W. Whitfield
                 118 Spring Street Northwest
                 Atlanta, Georgia  30304
```

603 APPEARANCE OF THE BUSINESS LETTER A business letter is usually typewritten on a sheet of paper 8½ by 11 inches. Double spacing is used between parts of the letter and between paragraphs. The typing should be so placed on the sheet as to have the margins properly proportioned, with the result that the typed text appears on the sheet much as does a picture properly set in a frame. Even when a letter conforms to all the other requirements of a good letter, its visual appearance also is important. The indented form (opposite) is optional in writing in longhand, but the block form is usual in typing (592). The semiblock style, in which the paragraphs are indented (usually five spaces), is used by many business houses. The following letter is in the semiblock style (592):

```
                            126 Park Place
                            Torrance, California   90507
                            May 12, 19--


Mr. J. D. Foster
1770 Pearl Street
Denver, Colorado   80202

Dear Mr. Foster:

     The information that you gave enabled me to
obtain the Greeley contract that I had feared could
not be concluded this spring.  It was generous of
you to take the trouble to assemble this data for me.

     As soon as I have checked the specifications,
I will see you for the final details.  You will agree
with me, I know, that the outlook is promising for us.

     Unless I meet with some unexpected delay, I
should have this preliminary work completed by the
end of the week.  I will let you know the day and the
hour to expect me.

                         Sincerely yours,

                         L. W. Whitman

LWW:pb                   L. W. Whitman
```

```
                          126 Park Place
                          Torrance, California   90507
                          May 12, 19--


Mr. J. D. Foster
   1770 Pearl Street
   Denver, Colorado   80202

Dear Mr. Foster:

        The information that you gave enabled me to
```

```
        end of the week.   I will let you know the day and the
        hour to expect me.

                          Sincerely yours,

                          L. W. Whitman

LWW:pb                    L. W. Whitman
```

604 COMMON TYPES OF BUSINESS LETTERS   There are business letters appropriate to all phases of business; therefore it would be almost impossible to classify all types. Only the commonly used types can be discussed in a brief book such as this. The following types of business letters are common: application, order, inquiry and reply, recommendation, introduction, claim, adjustment, acknowledgment and appreciation, advice, collection, congratulation, sales.

605 LETTER OF APPLICATION   This letter should conform to all requirements of a good business letter (589), and in form (590–603) it should be correct in every detail. No one should do less than one's very best in writing a letter of application. It is in reality a self-sale letter (615) in which the writer is trying to sell services. A short letter of application may consist of three or four paragraphs. The first may mention the source of information about the position, the second may give facts that indicate one's qualifications for holding the position, the third may list references, and the fourth may suggest a possible conference or further communication. But even the conventional form of application may be altered to suit the originality of the writer and the type of position sought. The more individual the message, providing it is always sincere and sensible, the more evident the fitness to fill a position requiring originality.

                                        1735 Magnolia Avenue
                                        Dallas, Texas 75201
                                        October 10, 19__

Miss Joan Hamilton
1917 Houston Street
Dallas, Texas 75201

Dear Miss Hamilton:

        I have just learned from Mr. Jones, one of
your salespeople, that you wish to employ a reliable
person to help with deliveries and to do odd jobs
about the store after school hours and on Saturdays.
I would like very much to have you consider me for
this work.

        I am fourteen years old and am now in the
ninth grade. For three summers I have been with
the Gray Drug Company as delivery boy and general
helper. You may ask Mr. H. W. Gray, the president
of this company, about my qualifications. His
telephone number is 283-8142.

        Also, I refer you to Principal H. G. White of
Lowell High School, where I am now a student, and
to Principal W. B. Lake of Roosevelt Junior High
School, the school from which I transferred last
January.

        I should be very happy to talk with you. My
telephone number is 314-3657.

                        Yours very truly,

                        Harold Roberts

                        Harold Roberts

606 ORDER The letter ordering goods should be made so clear that it
cannot possibly be misunderstood. It should be exact and complete in
every detail as to quantity, quality, size, catalog number, shape,
style, color, prices, or other items (as a sample of paper or cloth) helping toward exact identification. If the buyer is to pay transportation
charges, he should specify how the order is to be shipped—mail, air-
mail, express, freight, air freight—unless he leaves this matter to the
shipper and so states. The order should give complete instructions for
shipping. Printed order blanks may be used, but in any case no words
should be written in addition to those giving the items and exact instructions relating to the order. Write each item on a separate in-

dented line. If payment is enclosed, state the exact amount and the form in which it is sent—stamps, currency, check, draft, or money order. An enclosure, best placed in a blank envelope or fold of paper, may be stapled to the letter, but paper clips should not be used. In the lower left-hand corner should be written *Enclosure, Encl.,* or *Enc.*

grant school

1 PARK AVENUE · INDIANAPOLIS, INDIANA 20461 · SE 4-5643

January 10, 19--

McCormick-Mathers Publishing Company
300 Pike Street
Cincinnati, Ohio 45202

Dear Sir or Madam:

Please send me the following books and the tests
and other materials that accompany them by freight,
shipping charges collect:

41 PLAIN ENGLISH 1 at $1.71	$70.11
36 PLAIN ENGLISH 2 at $1.71	$61.56
32 PLAIN ENGLISH 3 at $1.71	$54.72
30 PLAIN ENGLISH 4 at $1.71	$51.30
109 PLAIN ENGLISH HANDBOOK	
Paperbound at $1.71	$186.39
30 PLAIN ENGLISH HANDBOOK	
Clothbound at $3.81	$114.30
	$538.38

Our check for $538.38 is enclosed.

Yours very truly,

J. D. Price

JDP:mb
Enclosure

J. D. Price, Principal

607 INQUIRY AND REPLY The letter of inquiry should state precisely what information is wanted. When properly expressed, there will be no need to have to write for a further explanation of any of its parts. The letter should be as brief as is consistent with courtesy and clarity. When the purpose of the inquiry is of no interest to the recipient, a stamped, self-addressed envelope should be enclosed for reply.

QUATOR PHARMACEUTICALS

2 ROCKEFELLER PLAZA, NEW YORK 10015

July 9, 19--

Mr. Fred Raner
Raner Drugstore
50 Lakewood Drive
Waco, Texas   76710

Dear Mr. Raner:

    Mr. J. H. Webb has applied for work as
a salesperson in my drugstore. He has referred
me to you as one for whom he has done similar
work. Please give me some general information
as to his fitness for this work. I shall be
grateful to you for this help.

Sincerely yours,

Lisa W. Stevens

LWS-PMB   Lisa W. Stevens

One who receives an inquiry should reply promptly unless it is the type of inquiry not in accord with business ethics. Even when the purpose of the inquiry is of no interest to the recipient, one should give the information as courteously and as fully as it it were of material benefit. One should give not only complete information for every detail of the inquiry but also any additional information which would be of help in the situation. In short, the writer should send the kind of reply he or she would wish for as the inquirer.

Answer to the letter on page 128.

Raner Drugstore

Phone: 817-9711   50 Lakewood Drive, Waco, Texas 76710

July 14, 19--

Ms. Lisa W. Stevens
Quator Pharmaceuticals
2 Rockefeller Plaza
New York, New York 10015

Dear Ms. Stevens:

    Mr. J. H. Webb has worked for me for two
years, and I found him thoroughly dependable
and efficient at all times. You may be sure
that he will give you excellent service. It
has been very difficult for me to find a salesperson of his ability to replace him since he
moved to your city. I shall appreciate any
consideration you show him.

                Yours sincerely,

                Fred Raner

FR/ss   Fred Raner

---

608 RECOMMENDATION   The letter of recommendation may be either personal or general. The personal type, such as the letter of reply above, is addressed to a person or firm by a writer who is recommending someone for a position. It may be written at the request of the one seeking the position or it may be in answer to an inquiry of the prospective employer. It should give concisely and clearly the information that would best help the employer in determining the applicant's fitness for the position.

There should be no vague statements and no overstressing of good qualities so as to make the applicant seem superhuman.

The general "To whom it may concern:" type of recommendation, that is placed in the hands of the one recommended, is seldom used today and it does not carry much weight because the tendency of its writer is to give only favorable facts. The employer of today prefers to send a questionnaire to references furnished by the applicant. In this way getting information which might be omitted from the general letter of recommendation. Of course, failure of a reference to answer the questionnaire or any item of it is interpreted as unfavorable to the candidate. The following, sent in answer to an inquiry, not containing a questionnaire, is an example of a longer recommendation than the preceding letter.

DOW INSURANCE

20 EAST 42ᵗʰ STREET • NEW YORK, N. Y. 10017 • OR 7-0110

June 12, 19--

Mrs. Deborah Jones
Central Insurance Company
1668 Blair Street
Louisville, Kentucky 40201

Dear Mrs. Jones:

It is with pleasure that we recommend Mr. F. H. Warren, about whom you inquire in your letter of June 10. He has been with us for five years, and in that time he has continued to grow in efficiency as an insurance salesperson until he is now among our largest and most consistent producers of quality business. It is because of this development that he now wishes to enter a larger field, such as you can offer him. We realize that his going will mean serious loss for us, but we do not wish to hold him back from the greater opportunities you can provide.

Mr. Warren is a persistent and tireless worker who considers rebuffs only as a challenge to lead him to improve his sales presentation. He is, we sometimes think, unduly impatient at his own reasonable progress; but this may be, after all, a commendable trait.

You will, we feel sure, find many occasions to consider yourselves fortunate if you engage Mr. Warren as a salesperson.

Sincerely yours,

C. C. Dow

C. C. Dow, President

CCD:ebe

609 **INTRODUCTION** The letter of introduction is used to introduce two of the friends or acquaintances of the writer. It may be given for either business or social reasons, but it should never be given except in all seriousness. One should never give a letter of introduction for business purposes unless one is absolutely sure of the ability and integrity of the person introduced. It would be much better to decline to give the letter than to give less than full approval of the person or to run the risk of introducing one not thoroughly competent and reliable. The message should be simple and as brief as is consistent with completeness and courtesy. The letter, delivered in person by the one introduced, should be enclosed in an unsealed envelope, bearing in proper position the name and full address of the one for whom it is intended and in the lower left-hand corner the words *Introducing Mr.* ——, *Mrs.* ——, or *Ms.* ——.

```
                          77 WEST 6 STREET
                          NEW YORK CITY  10024



                          1846 Oak Street
                          Springfield, Missouri  65801
                          October 6, 19--


Mr. F. L. Harper
1720 Market Street
St. Louis, Missouri  63155

Dear Mr. Harper:

     This will introduce you to Ms. Dale Holton, who
is seeking a position in your city. I have known
her for many years, and her training, ability, and
integrity fit her for excellent service in business
--the field in which she specialized in the University
of Missouri, from which she was graduated last June.

     For whatever courtesy or favor you may show this
young woman, both she and I will be grateful to you.

                          Sincerely yours,



     JKA:AB             James K. Atherton
```

610 **CLAIM** The letter of complaint or claim should always be courteous, dignified, and fair. It should state exactly the cause for complaint and should outline clearly the reasonable adjustment expected. The complainants who impute blame or become sarcastic or abusive only emphasize their own lack of refinement and make less probable the adjustment sought. If the impression is given that it is taken for granted that one is dealing with those who are absolutely honest and eager to make any reasonable adjustment, the complainant will seldom fail to get satisfaction. If one has had previous satisfactory dealings with the company, it is well to mention it to substantiate the expressed confidence. Most companies are quick to respond favorably to a justified complaint. The words *claim* or *complaint* are never used in such a letter.

3636 Weldon Street
Dallas, Texas   75201
May 6, 19—

The Glacier Book Company
340 Vine Street
Denver, Colorado   80202

Gentlemen:

On May the first I ordered from you one copy of Magic Mountain by Dale Warwick. The book arrived by mail today, and I found that some of the pages were transposed so that the book was not usable. I should like the privilege of returning the defective copy of the book to you in exchange for a perfect copy.

I shall wait for instructions from you.

You may be sure that I will appreciate your adjusting the matter for me.

Yours very sincerely,

H. C. Bradford

H. C. Bradford

---

611 ADJUSTMENT The writing of the letter of adjustment sometimes calls for much diplomacy. Those who write letters of complaint often do so while they are angry or in a disagreeable mood, but those who answer them should do so in such a way as to promote good feeling. Even when the complainant is very unreasonable and abusive, a reply showing courtesy and fairness is usually most effective. When the requested adjustment is to be made, the letter may be quite simple. An apologetic tone should be avoided, either expressed or implied.

GLACIER
BOOK CO. 340 Vine Street   Denver, Colorado   80202

May 8, 19--

Mr. H. C. Bradford
3636 Weldon Street
Dallas, Texas   75201

Dear Mr. Bradford:

    Thank you for calling our attention to the imperfect copy of <u>Magic Mountain</u>. We regret that you have been caused inconvenience, and we assure you that we are glad to adjust the matter. We are sending you by parcel post another copy of the work. We are enclosing with this letter postage for the return of the imperfect volume.

    We appreciate this opportunity of making our service satisfactory and hope to continue to be of service to you in the future.

Very truly yours,

L. W. Glade

LWG:EBK
Encl.

L. W. Glade
President

---

612 ACKNOWLEDGMENT OR ADVICE The receipt of an order or a remittance should be acknowledged at once. If the acknowledgment is of an order, it should refer to the date of the order with other definite reference, such as the order number if there is one, to identify it clearly. It should state when and how the order is to be shipped, and detailed explanation should be given if there is to be any delay in filling the order.

    Frequently a customer has ordered without having adequate information about the differences in the products available for shipment, which the acknowledgment must explain. If the order lacks necessary details, such as size, model, or other specifications, the writer of the acknowledgment should refer to the omission without showing impatience. In short, the acknowledgment should reflect sincere appreciation for the order and so foster a spirit of good will. An acknowledgment of a remittance should be made promptly, and it always should express that sincere appreciation which encourages further business relations. It often has elements of the sales letter (615). The letter of advice is one in which are enclosed the necessary shipping documents that pertain to an order (invoice, packing list, bill of lading, consular documents, bank draft, etc.); it also may be used to give details on the method and time of shipment. The following is an example of the letter of acknowledgment.

BELL 20 Office Park Drive, Birmingham, Ala. 35223
Sporting Goods

March 3, 19--

Mr. Robert Leewright
325 Central Drive
Lancaster, Pennsylvania 17601

Dear Mr. Leewright:

Thank you for your order of February 27 for our X214--7½-ft. spinning rod and L-340 spinning reel with 200 yards of 6-pound-test monofilament line. These will be shipped to you by express prepaid today.

You asked about our automatic reel A160 for fly rods. This will easily hold 25 yards of GAF line, but not 35 yards as you specify. May I suggest our A260 Automatic Reel, described in the enclosed circular? This is one of the finest reels on the market and has proved very popular. I believe it would fill the needs you indicate in your letter. The circular contains a convenient order form for your use.

Your order is very much appreciated, and we hope that we may continue to be of service to you.

Very truly yours,

Norma Roberts

NR:RM
Encl.

Norma Roberts
Sales Manager

VILIONS
DEPARTMENT STORE
4 EAST RIDGE AVENUE · WOOD, NEW JERSEY 07450
652-5252

October 18, 19--

Mr. J. F. G----
615 West Fifth Avenue
Wood, New Jersey 07450

Dear Mr. G----:

What do you think we should do?

We have a small account that remains unpaid. We
have sent two reminders. We are sincerely interested in keeping the good will of all our customers;
yet we cannot continue to build up a large collection
expense. What would you suggest that we do?

This small account is yours. It is only $46.28, but
it is six weeks overdue. You know the value of our
credit privilege, and I am sure you want to retain
it. Our spring sales will soon place a wide selection of fine bargains on our shelves, and you will
find your credit with us a valuable convenience.

Our extension of time on your account has already
been most liberal. In justice to our other customers
and as a matter of fair play, won't you settle this
account at once and retain your good credit standing?

I am enclosing an addressed, postage-free envelope
for your convenience. Please make use of it now to
send us your check. It will be appreciated.

Sincerely yours,

Olin Hiebert

OH:mr   Olin Hiebert
Enc.   Credit Manager

613 COLLECTION   The writer of the successful collection letter must use
tact. The task of collecting the money and of retaining the good will
and continued patronage of the customer is difficult. With all the
courtesy and consideration, however, the collector must not leave the
impression of being easygoing. Collectors should not be too friendly or
too sympathetic; and, above all, should not be apologetic. Firmness
should always be apparent.

614 CONGRATULATION   The message of congratulations in business need not be restricted by mere commercial relationships. It may be prompted more by courtesy than by obligation and it calls for no reply. It is of course very similar to the congratulatory letter of friendship (622), but it should follow the business-letter form, and its tone is often more formal, depending on the personal relationships involved. The following message is an example of this type of letter.

Newport Industries ⟋ 11 Broadway, New York, New York 10006

October 18, 19--

Mrs. Josephine Smith
4903 Ellis Avenue
Chicago, Illinois 60607

Dear Mrs. Smith:

As soon as I heard of your election to the
board of directors of your firm, I felt I must
write you to let you know how happy I am in
your advancement.

All of your friends have felt that, in spite
of the great difficulties you have faced in
your climb up through the ranks, the outstand-
ing ability we all recognized in you could not
go unacknowledged. This advancement is certainly
your due, and I think your firm should also be
congratulated on taking advantage more fully of
your exceptional talents.

Sincerely yours,

Charles E. Hodgson

Charles E. Hodgson
CEH:mr   President

Wimberly's Grill
90 Hanover Street, Palo Alto, California 94304

April 14, 19--

Mr. Gerald F. Bovell
1550 Fairmount Avenue
Palo Alto, California   94304

Dear Mr. Bovell:

Do you eat to live or live to eat?

Either way, you will enjoy eating at Wimberly's.
It goes without saying that the food is excep-
tionally fine. Only the choicest meats and
produce enter our kitchen, and we have long been
famous for the preparation of our foods. Have
you ever tasted our spare ribs? Try them--you've
never tasted anything so delectable.

Then, too, you'll enjoy the efficient, friendly
service at Wimberly's, the quiet decor, the
pleasant atmosphere.

Why not come in for lunch or dinner today? We'll
be glad to see you and we promise you the best
meal in town at a price still very modest.

Sincerely yours,

Robert Wimberly

RW:lr   Robert Wimberly
                     Manager

615 SALES   The sales letter is generally considered not only the most important of all business letters but also the most difficult to write. The
requirements of the business letter vary with individual types, but
every good sales letter must accomplish these four things: **attract attention, arouse desire, secure conviction,** and **induce action**—**brev-
ity,** the **"you" attitude,** and **completeness** are correlative with these
four. To do these things best, it should conform to all requirements
of the business letter (589). The good opening sentence in a sales
letter attracts the attention and causes the reader to continue reading.

Social Correspondence

616 SOCIAL LETTERS The social letter varies from the informal letter of
friendship to the most formal note. Social letters may be divided
into these groups: letters of **friendship, courtesy, formality.**

617 LETTERS OF FRIENDSHIP The letter of friendship may be light in tone
or dignified, and its style should be conversational (649). Even its
form is less conventional than that of the business letter, and the
stationery may vary to suit the taste of the writer. However, the general make-up is similar to that of the business letter, except that the
inside address (594) may be placed at the foot on the left side three
spaces below the signature. The **heading** (591), **salutation** (595),
complimentary close (599), **signature** (600), and **outside address**
(602) are similar to those of the business letter.

Because the letter of friendship is usually written in longhand,
some writers prefer to use the indented form (592) in the letter parts.
The punctuation (593) of the parts is the same as for the business
letter, except that a comma (instead of the colon) follows the salutation. The salutation, complimentary close, and signature are not so
formal; these should be in keeping with the relationship of the corre-
spondents. Such salutations as the following are appropriate: *Dear
Fred, Dear Mr. Hilton, Dear Aunt Mary.*

INFORMAL NOTE OF FRIENDSHIP:

> 6188 Maple St.
> Dallas, Texas 75201
> May 1 5, 19——

Dear Ruth,
It would be just great to hear from you! Of course you must be very
busy getting ready for college, but do let me know if you can spend the
last week in August with me before you leave. If you can come for my
birthday, August 31, you will be the best part of the celebration. I am
having a number of friends over that I would like you to meet.
I heard that you are going to be in a special pre-law program. You
always did have such a logical, well-organized mind!
With my interest in science, I've been thinking about a career in
medicine. Of course, I have a while to think about it, since I have another
year of high school.
Do you remember the playhouse in our yard? I've converted it into
a workroom where I've been doing pottery such as bowls and vases. You

must take one with you when you go to college. Please write and let me know your plans. I hope to see you soon.

Sincerely,

Betts

REPLY TO PRECEDING INFORMAL INVITATION:

1122 Maple Wood
Houston, Texas 77002
May 27, 19—

Dear Betts,

It was a nice surprise to get your letter. I was so busy with school and my part-time job at a department store that my correspondence got pushed aside. Thank you for your invitation to spend the last week in August with you. I would love to come. I can hardly wait to see you again! It would be lovely to meet your friends—I enjoy social occasions, especially birthday parties. We have a lot to talk about, from career plans to hobbies, and I am just counting the weeks until our visit.

Fondly,

Ruth

There are some points of the informal letter on which writers are not agreed. For instance, some omit the inside address altogether while others place it at the left below the signature; some even omit the heading, although this is a practical reminder of the address.

618 LETTER OF COURTESY The letter of courtesy, as defined in Clark's *When You Write a Letter*, is "the letter written not in reply to another letter nor yet to elicit a reply of any sort, but simply as an act of politeness and thoughtfulness to acknowledge a kindness or an obligation or to let one's friends or acquaintances know that one was aware of their sorrows and their successes, of their comings and goings, and that one had a real personal interest in these." Of the many classes of letters of this kind, only these four need be discussed: **acknowledgment, appreciation, condolence,** and **congratulation.**

619 ACKNOWLEDGMENT OR THANKS There are many types of acknowledgment (612) which duty and courtesy demand of us. It is obligatory that we acknowledge receipt of a letter, a present, an unusual courtesy, a favor, an offer, a request, or an invitation. There are many persons, however, including many young people, who do not respond to this social obligation. They should know, though, that this failure of acknowledgment brands them as thoughtless or ungrateful.

Rosedale, California
July 15, 19——

Dear Mr. and Mrs. Moore,

You may be sure that I shall always continue to enjoy the week which I have just spent in your home with Louise. You did everything possible to make us happy. The parties, the picnics, and the lunches were all so delightful and gay that I can never thank you enough for all the trouble you took for us.

Mother and I are already counting the days until Louise will be here with us. Tell her that I will write to her tomorrow.

Sincerely,

Henry Jones

620 APPRECIATION There is perhaps no other form of letter that has greater possibilities of bringing joy to both writer and recipient than the letter of appreciation. Yet it is a type which is neglected, because we human beings seem more inclined to condemn than to praise. Dr. Clark (see 618) says, "When there is something which can be criticized adversely or found fault with we jump at it [letter writing] with alacrity, but when we meet something worthy of praise, we say nothing." The expression of appreciation should be simple and sincere, with no implication of flattery.

80 Federal Street
Boston, Massachusetts 02109
October 24, 19——

Dear Mrs. Webster,

Years ago when I was in your class in English, I became discouraged. You will never know just how discouraged I was when you came to my rescue. You saw hope for me when I knew only despair. You gave me renewed faith in myself, and I am writing now, after all these years, to thank you. But in my heart I have thanked you a million times, and now I wish you to know that to you I owe the success which I am enjoying.

In this mail I am sending you an autographed copy of my latest book, which is having a very good sale, and I wish you to remember as you read it that without your encouragement it would never have been written.

Gratefully yours,

Charles G. Martin

621 CONDOLENCE A letter of condolence (sympathy) should always be written in longhand. It should be short and reflect the sincerity of the writer. Avoid reference to death or sorrow. Often there is no occasion for a letter of condolence from young people, as letters sent by one's parents are usually adequate. But there are times when a young person may feel the need to send some expression of his own feelings in a simple note such as the following:

> Dear Fred:
>   My deepest sympathy goes to you in the loss of your mother. I shall always remember how friendly and encouraging she was to me when I came over to your house.
>
>   Most sincerely,
>
>   *Tom*

There are occasions when one person may be selected to write a letter of condolence for a group or class:

> Dear Mr. and Mrs. Smith:
>   The Ninth Grade has asked me to express to you our deepest sympathy and the feeling of loss we all have. Fred was a valued companion to all of us and we feel privileged to have known him.
>
>   Most sincerely,
>
>   *Mildred Mason*
>   Class president

622 CONGRATULATION Sincere, appropriate words at times of successful achievement make for greater happiness in both the business (614) and social world:

> 356 Cochran Road
> Lexington, Kentucky 40501
> February 20, 19—
>
> Dear Fred,
>   Your winning first place against such strong competition did not surprise me at all, but it did make me happy. I congratulate you, for I know it was hard work, not luck, that brought you victory.
>   Now that you have won first place in oratory in competition with representatives of the leading universities in the United States,

I wonder if those of that smart set would still brand you hillbilly, as they did when they tried to rule you out of that first contest. If you are a hillbilly, you are running true to form, for there have been other Kentucky hillbillies (seems to me one was called "Abe") who have been heard from.

If I did not know you as I do, I'd offer some advice about disposing of your old hat. But I know it still fits you—you are immune from "swelled head." You'll have to let me strut a little, too; I don't know any better.

Sincerely yours,

Jack

623 FORMAL INVITATION, ACCEPTANCE, REGRET The formal invitation is always written in the third person. It has neither heading, inside address, salutation, complimentary close, nor signature. Only a few abbreviations such as *Ms.*, *Mr.*, *Mrs.*, and *Dr.* are permitted. Numbers other than house numbers are written out. The response to the invitation must be written in the same rigid form and must contain the information given by it.

INVITATION:

Mr. and Mrs. Henry L. Black
request the pleasure of
Miss Mildred Ware's
company at dinner
on Wednesday evening, the fourth of June
at seven o'clock
421 Glendale Road

ACCEPTANCE:

Miss Mildred Ware
accepts with pleasure
Mr. and Mrs. Henry L. Black's
kind invitation for dinner
on Wednesday evening, the fourth of June
at seven o'clock

REGRET:

Miss Mildred Ware
regrets that she is unable to accept
Mr. and Mrs. Henry L. Black's
kind invitation for dinner
on Wednesday evening, the fourth of June

624 TELEGRAM The telegram should be as brief as is consistent with clearness, which is absolutely essential. Telegrams are costly, and every word over the minimum increases the cost; but the elimination of words at the expense of clearness is poor economy. In all domestic telegrams the date, address, and signature are sent without charge. Each word, long or short, is counted. Thus it is economical to use one long word when it conveys the idea of two or more short ones. Punctuation marks are sent free. The word *stop* may be used between sentences for clarity, but it is counted as one word each time it is used. A standard abbreviation like C.O.D. is counted as one word. When figures or mixed groups of figures, letters, and signs (as 65%) are used, each group of five is counted as one word. Mailgrams, cablegrams, and radiograms are counted by a somewhat different method.

```
        MUST SELL PROPERTY BY NOON TOMORROW.
        WIRE OFFER BY THEN.

        BEST CASH OFFER $100,000 STOP
        $10,000 BINDER IN MAIL
```

Newspaper Writing

625 Newspaper writing includes news stories, headlines, feature stories, interviews, editorials, announcements, syndicated columns, and miscellaneous articles.

626 NEWS STORY   The news story tells recent important or interesting events. It usually begins with a summarizing paragraph called the lead, which should answer most of these questions: *Who? When? Where? What? Why? How?* This paragraph should be accurate and concise, and it should contain the main facts so that the reader need not proceed further unless details are wanted, which are given in the order of their importance in the paragraphs following the lead. Some newspapers are beginning to break away from this conventional lead-paragraph technique.

627 SUGGESTIONS FOR WRITING NEWS

1. Accuracy is of first importance. Get all the facts right. Be especially careful to spell personal and place names accurately.

2. Tell the story simply. Use specific rather than general terms. Do not use unnecessary words.

3. Tell facts only, never let it reflect the opinions of the reporter or editor.

4. In quoting, use the exact words of the person quoted. Never quote anything which would imply ignorance on the part of the speaker unles there is a clearly justifiable reason for doing so. In short, one should use tact and common sense in writing news just as in other forms of writing.

5. In preparing copy, follow exactly the instructions provided by the editor. A newspaper or journal usually has a style sheet which tells

which of certain alternative correct spellings and forms of capitalization and punctuation have been adopted by the paper for its
own use.

628 HEADLINES Headlines tell the news in a few words and guide the
readers in finding the news they wish to read. The main facts of the
story should be emphasized in the headlines. Short words are preferable. Do not use *a, an,* and *the.* Headline writers must count the
letters in each line written and rewrite it until the length meets
specifications in the style sheet of the newspaper. The large headlines contain several sections, each of which is called a **deck.** The top
deck tells the most important fact. Each deck should have a verb, and
should never end with a preposition. The present tense (191) and the
active voice (184) are preferable.

629 FEATURE STORY The feature story includes a variety of types of writing other than the usual news stories; it may be a brief human-interest
story suggested by some event introduced as news, or a fashion fore-
cast, or a book or play review; or it may be a long, informative article
such as those that appear in Sunday magazine sections. Reporters
may use a more individual style in writing feature stories than in reporting news and may sometimes state their own impressions and feelings or use quotations. Feature stories are frequently distinguished by
headlines different from those used for news stories, or they may be
printed in boxes.

630 REPORT OF INTERVIEW One who intends to report an interview (see
648) should have clearly in mind the questions to be asked. These
questions should be asked tactfully and should be recorded accurately
the answers for later writing. As few notes as possible should be
taken in the presence of the one interviewed, and, for this reason, the
report ought to be written immediately after the interview. In the lead
of such a story, a quotation from the one interviewed may be used and
it must be verbatim and have, if at all possible, the approval of the
interviewee to avoid error. Also, the name should be featured as well
as some of the characteristics. The subject of the interview or its
purpose should likewise be featured.

631 EDITORIALS An editorial is an essay (640) on some subject of interest
to the public. All writers are free to use their own individual style. The
editorial usually has a title instead of headlines and a lead. Its purpose
is generally to present an argument, to entertain, or occasionally to
give information. The argumentative type is usually on a subject of
public interest and is often a plea for some reform. The facts upon
which such an argument is based should be carefully verified by reliable
authorities. The editorial which means to entertain is often a kind of
informal essay and is usually less serious in style than the other forms,

being sometimes satirical or humorous. Polemical writing is a style completely at variance with the intent and scope of good editorial writing.

THE BIRTHDAY OF WILL ROGERS

THIS is the birthday of one of the most beloved figures in all American history—Will Rogers. Unexpected tragedy took him from the scene of public life at the height of his activity and the pinnacle of his fame but had he lived to be a hundred or more he would have retained a warm spot in the hearts of millions of Americans.

Will was born, according to his own statements, at Oolagah, Indian Territory, but it was Claremore, Okla., that gained fame as his home town and Claremore has completed a shrine to its most famous son.

Will was listed in *Who's Who* as a humorist, but he was far more than that. He was a philosopher, a counsellor, a guide to millions of Americans who depended upon his daily bit of philosophy or whimsical humor to set them right with the world. Will had the faculty of pointing the way to the truth in a kindly way.

A sudden mishap of the air snuffed out the lives of Will Rogers and Wiley Post, another famous son of Oklahoma, up in the wilds of Alaska. Numerous monuments were raised in his honor, even before the completion of the memorial at Claremore, but the greatest memorial is the niche the cowboy humorist of Oklahoma still retains in the hearts of millions.

An editorial in the Wichita *Beacon* on William Penn Adair Rogers (1879–1935), American actor and humorist.

632 ANNOUNCEMENTS   A form of writing for publication which is important but not extensive is the announcement, which should be brief, clear, emphatic, and free from exaggeration. Kipling's six honest serving men (p. 115) will prove helpful in the writing of announcements.

The Research Paper

633 SOURCE MATERIAL   Choose a subject in which you are interested and which is not too broad in scope. Once you have chosen your subject, consult the Card Catalog and *Reader's Guide to Periodical Literature* in your library to find out what reference material is available. Note the copyright date; some of the material may be out of date for your purpose.

Keep in mind the difference between original and secondary sources of material. For example, in writing about a person, letters would be an original source of information, and a printed collection of letters will generally be as good as an original source (keeping in mind the fact that letters may have sometimes been edited in a reprint edition). A secondary source would be the opinions of another author about the person under discussion. For important papers, original sources should be used when available.

634 THE SOURCE CARD TECHNIQUE List each source on a separate card—usually 3 x 5 inches. Include—

1. **Author's name.** Give last name first, then given names, or the editor's name followed by the abbreviation *Ed.* When no author is given, list the title first.

2. **Title.** Underline the title of a book, magazine, or newspaper and put quotation marks around the title of an article or chapter.

3. **Publication data.** For book titles include the city where published, name of publisher, and copyright date. For magazines or journals use the volume number, date of issue, and page numbers.

4. **Library call number.** For books include the call number so that you don't have to look this up again. Here are samples of source cards for a book, an article in a magazine, and an article in an encyclopedia:

> 610 Williams, Roger J.
> W   Threat against Disease,
>   Environmental Prevention,
>   New York: Pitman Publishing
>   Corporation, 1971

> Young, Gordon, "Pollution,
> Threat to Man's Only Home."
> National Geographic,
> Vol. 138, No. 6, December, 1970,
> pp. 738-780

> "Ecology," Encyclopedia
> International, 1970 edition,
> Vol. 6, pp. 205-208

635 OUTLINES Start with a working outline showing clearly the topics you expect to write about. As you gather material, you may want to change this outline, omitting some topics about which you find little source material and adding others that appear to be interesting or more significant. After you have gathered all your information, you may make your final outline (579–80) to guide your writing.

636 TAKING NOTES The best way to gather material is to take notes on 3 x 5 inch or larger cards for which you have a file box. These cards will enable you to organize your material and refer readily to your information on each topic as you write. The following are helpful rules for taking notes:

1. **Use a separate card for each note.** This permits you to file your cards under the proper topic. Sometimes more than one card will be necessary for a topic.

2. **Take thorough notes on all of the points you plan to cover.** Many students find that three or four good notes are required for every page of the research paper. Don't keep repeating information even if it is found in different books, and do not take notes on material you do not plan to use.

3. **List the topic the note refers to.** The topic is best placed at the top left corner of the card. This enables you to refer to your notes quickly as you write and helps you to organize your material.

4. **Be accurate.** Your notes must report facts, figures, opinions, and quotations accurately. Double-check every word and every figure with your source. Give enough detail so that you yourself can understand what you have written.

5. **Mark each direct quotation clearly.** Put quotation marks around each short quotation. Longer quotations are shown by leaving larger margins (510). Take down the exact words, punctuation, and capitalization. Use three dots to indicate the omission of parts of a quotation (488). Use direct quotations only if you plan to give the exact opinion of an authority or if the same idea cannot possibly be expressed in your own words. Too many quotations will make a very weak paper. Express your own ideas in your own way.

6. **Identify the source and give the page reference for each note.** This information will be necessary for your footnotes (638) and your bibliography (639). You should have some key for connecting your note card with its source card. You may make up your own abbreviation for each source card, or you may number your source cards in order and then put the proper source number on each note card.

637 WRITING THE PAPER When you have your purpose and viewpoint clearly in mind, you may start by writing an introduction. Otherwise, save your introduction to the last and start with your first topic. Follow your final outline in arranging your notes. In this way your material will be logically organized, but you still must supply transitions (549)—sometimes using whole paragraphs—to make your paper a unified, coherent whole. Try to make your sentences sound smooth and connected, not a miscellaneous assortment hastily thrown together. A first draft may be written rapidly, but be very careful of the mechanics of your writing in your revised final copy.

638 **Footnotes** General information—such as you have found in a number of different books—usually doesn't have to be credited. But specific information—statistics, direct quotations, opinions of experts— should be credited. You give credit in two ways. If the source is clear, you may mention it briefly in a sentence within your paragraph: "As H. C. Lodge says in *Science* for May 22, 1977, . . ." But usually a footnote is best for complete reference to your source. At the end of material to be credited, put a number slightly above the line to correspond to the number you will use for your footnote at the bottom of the page. Numbers usually run consecutively throughout an entire paper, but it is not incorrect to start over with each new page.

Material to be credited should be taken accurately from your note cards, and you can take from your source cards all the data necessary for your footnote credit. The following are examples of forms you may use for articles and books. Since you will have a full bibliography, you may omit publication data from your footnotes if your teacher approves.

Book

> [1]
> Robert Wells, Electronics, Key to Exploring Space. (New York: Dodd, Mead & Company, 1964), p. 125.

Magazine article

> [2] E. M. Shoemaker, "Moon Close Up," National Geographic, Vol. 126 (November 1964), pp. 690-707.

Encyclopedia article

> [3]"Space Science and Exploration," Collier's Encyclopedia, 1971 edition, Vol. 21, pp. 343-380.

When you refer several times to the same source, it is not necessary to repeat the entire footnote. Suppose you need to credit an article the second time before you refer to any other source. Simply write *Ibid.* (meaning "in the same place") as your footnote, adding a page number if the page is different:

> [4]Ibid., p. 71.

Some writers use *Loc. cit.* (in the place cited) when the page number is the same. If another footnote has intervened, write the author's name and *op. cit.* ("in the work cited"), or just use the author's name:

⁵Wells, op. cit., p. 71.   ⁵Wells, p. 71.

If the author is not given, a shortened reference to the previous source may be used:

⁶Collier's Encyclopedia, p. 352.

639 BIBLIOGRAPHY At the end of your research paper give a bibliography of all the printed material you have used in preparing your paper. Usually your bibliography will include the same works that you credited in your footnotes, but you may list additional helpful works that you consulted but did not have to credit. The form of your bibliographical entries is the same as that in your source cards. These should be alphabetized and copied accurately.

Newlon, Clarke, A Thousand and One Questions Answered About Space, Revised Edition. New York: Dodd, Mead & Company, 1971.

Shoemaker, E. M., "Moon Close Up," National Geographic, Vol. 126 (November 1964), pp. 690-707.

"Space Science and Exploration," Collier's Encyclopedia, 1971 edition, Vol. 21, pp. 343-380.

Wells, Robert, Electronics, Key to Exploring Space. New York: Dodd, Mead & Company, 1964.

Writing Essays

640 ESSAYS The term *essay* is a rather broad one, for it includes all forms of short creative writing inspired by personal reactions. Inexperienced writers, however, should restrict their attempts at essay writing to one type—the informal, or familiar, essay. This form is the expression of the writer's own thoughts on his chosen subject. The subject and the style of the informal essay may vary to suit the writer. The style of the writing, though, is in keeping with the mood of the theme. Some suggestions offered for writing the informal essay are: *make your reader share your ideas and understand their relation, choose appropriate words, use a simple style, use quotations and figures of speech, vary your sentences, revise for clearness and effectiveness.*

Oral Communication

641 Oral communication is made up largely of conversation, the most informal of the types of communication; but it includes speaking in public, which may vary greatly in its degree of formality.

Conversation

642 Conversational language is normally less formal than that which is written, even in letters; but the conversationalist meets with dangers not encountered by the writer. Here are some suggestions for those who would like to be good conversationalists:

1. **Be a good listener.** Perhaps there is no more effective way of gaining the reputation of being a good conversationalist than by listening attentively. Be interested and never interrupt.

2. **Get the other's viewpoint.** Do your best to see things as the other person sees them. This is not easy but it is important.

3. **Learn the other person's interests.** Show interest in the other's interests, not just in expressing your own.

4. **Respect the opinions of others.** Though you may not agree with another person's opinions, respect that person's right to have them.

5. **Never argue.** There is nothing to gain by arguing in ordinary conversation, but there is much to lose.

6. **Make no reference to the other person's weakness.**

7. **Acknowledge excellence in others.** All people have superior points that deserve recognition.

8. **Stimulate the other's feeling of importance.** Honestly and sincerely encourage the other's self-respect.

9. **Say the other person's name.** But be sure to use the name naturally and not as if for effect, and be doubly sure to pronounce it correctly. No one ever quite forgives the person who mispronounces or misspells one's name.

10. **Do not be a know-it-all.** Perhaps the most unpopular of all conversationalists is the know-it-all—the person who tops every tale, no matter how tall—the person who boasts about having been everywhere and seen everything.

11. **Do not be gloomy.** Do not dwell on mournful or depressing incidents or predictions. Try at least to appear cheerful and hopeful.

12. **Do not be cynical.** Refrain from expressing the views of a disparager—a doubter—an unbeliever in sincerity or nobility.

13. **Never be catty.** Those who make catty (slyly spiteful—as the dictionary says) remarks cannot hope to have friends.

14. **Do not be overcorrect.** Use good but natural speech, and do not overdo correctness by becoming finicky about unimportant usages. In your community use the language of your community.

15. **Be genuinely courteous.** Be tactful and courteous always. In a group, make everyone feel at ease. Include everyone in your conversation, and do not talk over the heads of anyone present. Encourage those who are reticent or shy. They may often be the most interesting talkers.

16. **Be able to make correct introductions.** One should be able to introduce oneself and to introduce others properly and tactfully. Any good book on etiquette will serve to refresh one's memory on special points of introduction, but ordinarily one can easily remember that the boy is presented to the girl, the man to the woman, and the younger person to the older person. John Jones may introduce himself to another by saying, "I am John Jones." He may introduce two others, a boy and a girl, by saying, "Mildred Gray, this is Bob Jones." If Bob is seated, he rises at the introduction and says, "How do you do?" Mildred may or may not offer to shake hands nor need she rise if seated. Usually people, on being introduced, shake hands. The forms of introductions are more or less fixed, but informality need not be ruled out.

Speaking Before an Audience

643 Few of us become professional public speakers, but there are occasions in the life of everyone when the ability to address an audience effectively is highly advantageous. General suggestions include those on the appearance of the speaker, the voice, the language, the preparation of the speech, and the delivery:

1. **Appearance of the Speaker.** The speaker should be neatly and appropriately dressed. In facing the audience, one should assume an air of dignity and poise. After a slight pause, through which one stands in an easy, natural position, one should begin to talk. One should look at one's audience without special attention to individuals. One should become so much absorbed in the message that one's hands and feet will not seem awkward appendages. If notes are used, they should be typed on small cards, so that they may be glanced at without attracting the attention of the audience.

2. **Voice.** The speaker should use natural tones and should speak loudly enough to be heard distinctly by all. If there is a microphone, speak directly toward it. The voice should be well modulated with no tendency toward monotonous singsong. Every word should be pronounced correctly (675) and clearly, without any semblance of affectation.

3. **Language.** Use correct language in speaking before an audience, especially in giving a formal address before a dignified audience. In such an audience there are sure to be those who associate errors in speech with ignorance. In the less formal type of talk, of course, one may, as in conversation, use a style less dignified and precise. Surely one who addresses an audience of close friends should take advantage of the privilege, permissible in informal conversation, of using moderate amounts of slang to lend color to one's expression. Tact, that great aid in all situations

in life, is never more suitably employed than in the language of the public speaker. The speaker possessed of an adequate vocabulary, common sense, tact, and a good message can win the attention of any audience.

4. **Preparation of the Speech.** In preparing a speech, one usually has in mind to instruct, to convince, or to entertain. Accordingly every part of the speech should be appropriate to its purpose. It should also be appropriate to the occasion on which it is given and to the audience. The speaker shouldn't memorize the address, although it should have been carefully outlined in notes. The outline should consist of an introduction, main message, and conclusion.

5. **Delivery of the Speech.** Be sure that your beginning is forceful. The first sentence often determines the whole effect of an address. Never begin a speech with an apology. No matter how poorly prepared you are, never apologize. If jokes or humorous stories are used, be sure they have a purpose and that they are appropriate. If you cannot tell a joke well, omit it. One butchered joke will spoil the effect of a good speech. Be sincere, and above all, be enthusiastic—enthusiasm is contagious. There is no excuse to drone—to speak listlessly and disinterestedly—a speech even in a good cause, for it always hurts the cause it should promote. Be sure to stop promptly when your message is ended. In making an announcement, be brief; but make sure your announcement is fully understood.

Other Forms of Oral Communication

644 THE TELEPHONE Only general suggestions for the use of the telephone may be offered here:

1. Be sure to exercise the same courtesy and consideration in using the telephone that you would if you were talking directly with the person. This means, of course, that the voice should be properly modulated and that there must be no indication of indifference, inattention, hurry, impatience, or annoyance.

2. Be alert, responsive, and courteous under even the most trying circumstances.

3. The person responsible for the telephone conversation should terminate it. Therefore it is impolite for the one called to conclude the conversation unless there is good reason for doing so.

4. Do not prolong a telephone conversation on trivial matters when someone is waiting to use the telephone.

5. Do not use a business telephone for prolonged personal visiting.

6. Do not use another's private telephone without asking permission.

7. Do not, by distracting noise or actions, disturb someone who is using a telephone.

8. Never eavesdrop when someone is using the telephone. Furthermore, it is discourteous to question someone about something that you happen to overhear in a telephone conversation with another person.

645 ORAL BOOK REPORT The oral book report seems to be growing in popularity in clubs and other organizations outside the schools. Those who learn to make effective book reports in school may, therefore, find their training very useful in maturer years. There are few definite rules for making a book report: first name the book; its author, its publisher, its time of publication and then:

1. Explain something of the purpose of the book.

2. Tell something of the characters and the setting (when reviewing fiction).

3. Compare the work with others of a similar nature.

4. Read brief extracts from the book to indicate its style; but they should be carefully selected and read well. (Do not read without prior practice with the text.)

5. Explain why you do or do not like the book.

6. Use good English without being bookish. Make your report clear and enjoyable.

646 STORYTELLING Storytelling at its best is a fine art. Few of us, of course, become artists in this field; but everyone should learn to tell stories at least reasonably well. In addition to the suggestions offered under 643, there are others which good story-tellers follow, such as these:

1. Plunge immediately into the story.

2. Give the events in their logical order.

3. Vary your sentence structure, and put life into your expression.

4. Suit your mood to that of the story, but remember that tactful humor is seldom inappropriate.

5. Make your conclusion strong—imagination will help you to an impressive close.

647 ANECDOTES Everyone should learn to tell anecdotes well. A bit of artful humor lends tang to any conversation, and the effectiveness of a public speaker often depends on one's skill at using appropriate anecdotes. Here are a few general suggestions:

1. The anecdote should be suited to the listeners and to the occasion.

2. It should be brief.

3. It should have a point, revealed only with the conclusion—the punch line as it is called. Have clearly in mind the exact wording of your final sentence.

4. Use common sense in your selection of anecdotes.

5. Tell your anecdote *effectively* once, but don't repeat any part of it.

6. Don't suggest that maybe your audience has heard the story before.

648 INTERVIEW An interviewer should introduce himself or herself and then make clear the purpose of the meeting. If the interviewee is seeking a position, all qualifications should be stated frankly, accurately, and confidently without seeming boastful. After the meeting the interviewee should thank the interviewer, whether the outcome of the interview is favorable or not.

649 DISCUSSION Friendly, intelligent discussion is one of the most enlightening forms of communication. Your teacher will help you plan interesting discussions in class. There is no lack of excellent subjects for such discussion: community affairs, current events, a story, a play, a poem, or some popular book.

In a good discussion everyone is interested and everyone wants to talk. Everyone has studied the topic and has something to say. There will be strong opinions and perhaps some excitement. This is as it should be; a discussion should be fun and should lead to self-expression. This does not mean that loss of temper or rude interruption is an acceptable form of self-expression. Excitement does not excuse discourtesy. Loud argument and squabbles destroy discussion. The following are suggested rules for good discussion.

1. Choose a topic of real interest to the group.

2. Give everyone a chance to talk.

3. Listen to what others say so that you can contribute to the line of discussion. Avoid repeating what someone else has said.

4. Stick to the subject.

5. Don't interrupt.

6. Show respect for others' opinions, but don't be shy in expressing your own opinion.

7. Be courteous in correcting a statement you think is an error.

8. Don't argue about facts; look them up.

To make sure that everyone who wishes to talk has a fair chance, the group should have a chairperson. The discussion may be largely informal, but all students should "address the chair" and wait until the chairperson speaks their names. This procedure avoids the unprofitable situation in which everyone tries to talk at once. A good chairperson will also keep the speakers on the subject.

650 GIVING INFORMATION People should train themselves to ask for and to give information briefly, accurately, and courteously. In giving information, as for instance, on how to find a place, it is often necessary to repeat for emphasis; but too much repetition confuses.

651 ANNOUNCEMENTS AND BRIEF TALKS Everyone should be able to make clear, effective announcements and to make creditable short talks before audiences. Every student should be able to announce effectively a coming event, make a rousing pep talk, introduce a speaker, or make a nomination or a presentation speech. In all these one should remember to stick to the main purpose, be brief, give facts, and make a strong beginning and closing.

652 CLUBS AND OTHER ORGANIZATIONS Work in organized groups in schools is so familiar to students that detailed instructions are not needed here. You have, no doubt, taken part in many school organizations. Under the guidance of your teacher, you have become familiar with the working rules of groups. If there are points on which you are not clear, any standard work, such as *Robert's Rules of Order, Revised, The Sturgis Standard Code of Parliamentary Procedure*, or L. W. Bridge, *Book of Parliamentary Procedure*, will set you right. A summary of the essential rules for regular club work would include these: *How to call a meeting to organize a group, how to nominate and select officers, how to make a motion, how to second a motion, how to call a meeting to order, how committees are appointed, how the chairperson of a committee is selected.* A knowledge of these rules coupled with good judgment and consideration for others will enable you to do effective, enjoyable club work.

7

Choice of Words

"The old Knight laughed exultantly. 'Here is a pupil who never brings me shame! . . . Hark ye! only last week that young jock-fool, the young Lord of Brocas, was here talking of having seen a covey of pheasants in the wood. One such speech would have been the ruin of a young squire at court. How would you have said it, Nigel?' . . . 'Surely, fair sir, it should have been a nye of pheasants.' " Quoted from Sir Arthur Conan Doyle's novel *Sir Nigel.*

Standards of Diction

653 LANGUAGE IS GROWING   A living language is constantly changing. Its standards of correctness are established by those who are considered its most authoritative users. Inexperienced writers and speakers especially should stay within the limits of those standards and use only words which are sanctioned by best authority. However, this standard of correctness may vary with the form of expression in which it is found. The formal literary type of expression would be out of place in a more informal situation requiring a colloquial (647) type of expression. The report of a football game kept to the standard required for a formal essay would no doubt be rather dull reading. Even the standard required for the less formal kinds of writing might be altogether out of place in conversation.

Good English is that which is appropriate to the type of expression in which it is used. Diction as used here refers to the choice of words for accuracy, clarity, variety, and effectiveness rather than to its second meaning, the manner of the speaking, that is, the pronunciation and enunciation of public speakers and singers.

Varieties of Diction

654 There are types of expressions which are avoided by the best writers and speakers. But there are other types of word usage that are perfectly acceptable when appropriate to the situation. An understanding of this appropriateness marks the educated person. Most types of word usage may be classified under the following headings: **archaic expressions, barbarisms, colloquialisms, improprieties, neologisms** (newly coined words), **provincialisms, slang, vulgarisms, hackneyed** or **trite expressions**, and **idiomatic expressions**.

655 ARCHAIC EXPRESSIONS Words are archaic which have become old-fashioned and no longer are used naturally: *spirituous* (for *spirited*), *eftsoons* (for *soon after*), *methinks, avaunt.*

> ARCHAIC: The youthful crowd will be *convocated* here *anon.*
> MODERN: The young people will gather here soon.

656 BARBARISMS Word distortions, such as *alright, complected, disremember, irregardless* are to be avoided in contemporary usage.

> BARBARISM: I *disremember* the incident.
> STANDARD: I do not remember the incident.

657 COLLOQUIALISMS Some expressions are correctly used in informal conversation or in informal writing that are not appropriate in formal composition. The ordinary contractions, such as *doesn't, hasn't,* and *can't,* are examples of colloquialisms. The modern colloquial style of writing requires great skill except when it reflects reported speech.

> COLLOQUIAL: *It's funny* that he *doesn't* return.
> FORMAL: It is strange that he does not return.

658 IMPROPRIETIES Good words may be used inappropriately, such as *set* for *sit, most* for *almost, accept* for *except, affect* for *effect:*

> IMPROPRIETY: It seems that *most all* the students are here.
> CORRECT: It seems that almost all the students are here.

659 NEOLOGISMS Large numbers of words are added to the language or changed in meaning each year, and they are not necessarily to be avoided. When in doubt, check with an up-to-date dictionary.

RECENTLY COINED: Have you heard about the *recycling* of waste materials?

Fred read about *soul music*.

Jane was undecided about her new dress: *mini, midi,* or *maxi?*

660 PROVINCIALISMS Dialectal words, often nonstandard and used by local people, are expressions peculiar to a region (province), such as *carry* (for accompany), *poke* (for bag or sack), *cayuse* (for range horse), *jolt wagon* (for farm wagon).

PROVINCIAL: She cooked a meal in the *spider.*

GENERAL: She cooked a meal in the frying pan.

661 SLANG Are you a "square"? Or is square (to describe a person) so outdated that you would call anyone who used it a "turkey"? Both are terms of scorn; *square* is given in some dictionaries as a slang term to refer to a person who does not fit in with the "in" group; Turkey has reached the dictionary as slang but may already have disappeared from teenage language. Most slang is overworked and quickly worn to threads.

Slang may be the language of your group, but usually it would be wise not to use it in writing or in talking with older people. Adults may have at one time in their lives used a great deal of slang, but they know how tiresome and meaningless it may become. Still, slang is clever, forceful, or picturesque and may sometimes become part of the language of mature people—such words as *sob story, mob,* or *stooge* are now accepted. Slang should not be entirely despised, but it should be used with care.

Various terms are associated with slang in describing non-standard usage: **dialect, patois, argot, jargon, cant, vernacular.** Each has its own particular application. See your dictionary.

662 VULGARISMS Some words are never correct in either formal or informal expression: words such as *blowed, brung, busted* (for burst), *drawed, drownded, et, growed, hain't, hern, hisn, hisself, knowed, nowheres, scairt, theirn, theirselves, them there,* and *this here.* The term also applies to obscenities.

663 HACKNEYED OR TRITE EXPRESSIONS Phrases that have been over-used until they have almost lost their effectiveness are **trite.** Although young writers are tempted to use these worn-out expressions or clichés, they should learn to substitute more vital ones. Some of the hackneyed terms frequently used are *brave as a lion, brown as a berry, busy as a bee, cold as ice, green as grass, pearls before swine.*

664 Idiomatic Expressions Idioms are expressions that are peculiar to every language and often they are not governed by the rules of its grammar; therefore it is difficult to translate them into another language. Idioms, though they may defy analysis within the rules of grammar, have nevertheless become through long-continued usage firmly established as standard.

That these expressions at first glance may not be parsed or diagrammed should not discourage their use. The very best writers of all languages make constant use of idioms. Some common English idioms are *put up with, all of a sudden, get rid of it, in the long run, get into hot water, with a grain of salt.* Be careful to use correct idioms. The prepositions especially are often determined by their idiomatic use rather than by logic:

UNIDIOMATIC: Hal was accompanied *with* his brother.
CORRECT: Hal was accompanied by his brother. (See 355.)

Usage Glossary

665 Some of the expressions listed here are in established use in **informal speech and writing**, but standard usage calls for the more **formal expression in writing**. Remember, however, that usage changes. Learn to check with the dictionary.

666 Accept—except. *Accept* means *to take* or *receive.* *Except* (verb) means *to exclude* or *leave out.* As a preposition it means *but* or *excluding.*

I *accept* a gift.
We voted to *except* these members from service.
All the gifts *except* yours were returned.

Act. When used as a linking verb to mean "seem" or "pretend to be," *act* is followed by an adjective:

He certainly *acted* stupid.

Affect—effect. *Affect* is a transitive verb meaning *to influence* or *to pretend. Effect* as a verb means *to bring about; effect* as a noun means *result*:

The noise *affects* (not *effects*) my hearing.
They *effected* (not *affected*) a compromise.
His work had a good *effect* (not *affect*).

All right. Use the phrase *all right* rather than *alright*; the latter word is recorded but, as yet, with little approval for use.

Is it *all right* (not *alright*) to take the car?
Already—all ready. *Already* is the adverb:

The guests had come *already*.

We were *all ready* for the fun.

Alternative. This word means a *choice between two things*.

He had the *alternative* of resigning or of being fired.

Altogether—all together. *Altogether* is the adverb:

This is *altogether* bad.

They were *all together* in the boat.

A one. It is archaic to use *a* with *one* in a sentence like this:

There was not *one* (not *a one*) who would volunteer.

As. After verbs of *saying, knowing, thinking,* or *feeling,* do not use *as* for *whether* or *that* (379). (See also 371 and 381.)

I do not know *that* (not *as*) I can go.

So—as, as—as. In negative statements use the correlatives *so—as;* in positive statements use *as—as:*

He is not *so* tall *as* John.

He is *as* tall *as* John.

At. Do not use *at* unnecessarily with *where:*

Where is the book *at?* (Omit *at.*)

667 **Awful.** This term originally meant *awe-inspiring,* but it has been so weakened by its colloquial use that it can seldom be used in its original meaning. *Awful* and *awfully* should be avoided in most writing since they are merely general terms of emphasis or disapproval:

Jane is *unusually* (not *awfully*) smart.

This was a *difficult* (not an *awful*) job.

Badly. In formal writing do not use this adverb in the sense of *very much* nor as a predicate adjective (289)

I want *very much* (not *badly*) to succeed.

He looks *bad* (not *badly*) since his illness.

Complected. This is a barbarism.

She is *light-complexioned* (not *light-complected*).

Compliment—complement. A compliment expresses *praise;* a complement *completes something:*

She paid him a sincere *compliment.*

The verb mentioned has two *complements.*

Considerable. Use this term as an adjective; rarely as a noun.

A *considerable* sum of money is invested in that plant.

They have done *considerable* for the school. (informal)

668 **Credible—credulous.** Credible means *believable;* credulous means *believing too easily:*

That is a *credible* story.

He was too *credulous* in accepting their account.

Disremember. This word is not standard though marked *colloquial* or *informal* in some dictionaries:

I do not *remember* (not I *disremember*) his name.

Either—neither. Best used to indicate one of two persons or things:

None (not *neither*) of the four boys would go.

Either of the *two* girls can take the part.

Neither of the *two* plans were approved.

669 Enthused. Although classed as colloquial by some dictionaries, it is shunned in good writing.

He is *enthusiastic* (not *enthused*) about the plan.

Expect. In formal writing do not confuse *expect*, meaning *to anticipate*, with *suppose*, meaning *to be of the opinion*:

I *suppose* (not *expect*) he is wealthy.

We *expect* to see you tomorrow.

Farther—further. The distinction between *farther* to refer to *spatial distance* and *further* to refer to *time, degree,* or *quantity* is waning but it is still observed by many careful writers:

We walked *farther* than two miles.

I shall go no *further* with this business.

The explorer went *further* into the forest.

Fix. This is colloquial when used to mean *predicament, difficult situation,* or *condition* and badly overused:

I was in a desperate *situation* (not *fix*) about my grades.

Formally—formerly. *Formally* means *in a formal manner; formerly* means *previously*:

The guest was treated *formally*.

He was *formerly* mayor of the town.

Funny. Do not use for *odd* or *strange*, except in colloquial expressions:

It is *strange* (not *funny*) that he lost his fortune.

Gentleman—lady. These terms are sometimes applied to show respect but are more often merely pretentious. Of course, in addressing an audience the speaker still may correctly say: "Ladies and gentlemen." The terms *man* and *woman* are best for general use:

I met a pleasant woman (not *lady*) at the museum.

Get up. This two-word verb in the meaning of *organize, prepare,* or *arrange,* is now acceptable for general use though it is informal in feeling.

They *got up* a good party for the team.

670 Good. Do not use the adjective *good* as an adverb (329):

He sings *well* (not *good*).

Got. *Got,* with *had, has,* or *have* to indicate possession or obligation emphatically, is generally acceptable.

He *has got* the money here.

I *have got* to go immediately.

Had ought to. Do not use *had ought to* for *ought to* or *should:*

You *ought* (not *had ought*) to write to Ned.

You *should* (not *had ought to*) read this book.

Imply—infer. A speaker or writer may *imply* more than he says, the hearer *infers* what the speaker intends:

We *inferred* from what Jim said that he was angry with us.

The speaker did not *imply* that anyone in particular was to blame.

Invite—invitation. It is still dialectal, after three hundred years of use, to use the word *invite* for the noun *invitation:*

She has an *invitation* (not *invite*) to the lecture.

Is where—is when. These terms should not be used in definitions:

Subtraction is *taking* (not *where* or *when you take*) one number from another.

671 Kind of—sort of. It is still better (though opinion varies) not to use these terms for *rather* or *somewhat* (333).

He seems *rather* (not *sort of* or *kind of*) tired.

Lay—lie. *Lay* is usually transitive and takes a receiver of its action; its principal parts are *lay—laid—laid. Lie* is intransitive in its usual meanings and does not take an object; its principal parts are *lie—lay—lain* (but see 217).

Did you *lay* (not *lie*) the rake on the ground?

You should not *lie* (not *lay*) on the wet grass.

Learn—teach. To *learn* means to *get knowledge;* to *teach* means to *give knowledge* (227).

You should *learn* to play tennis.

Teach me how to swim.

Less—fewer. *Less* refers to *quantity; fewer* refers to *number:*

This lake has *less* water than the other.

This tree has *fewer* branches than that.

Liable—likely. *Likely* means *probably; liable* means *responsible* for or it may refer to a *possibility with unpleasant results:*

He is *likely* (not *liable*) to win the race.

He is *liable* for his own debts.

He is *liable* to harm someone.

Like. In formal writing do not use *like* for *as, as if,* or *as though,* in introducing a clause:

Do *as* (not *like*) I do.

He acted *as if* (not *like*) he knew it and *as though* (not *like*) he had always known it.

Mad. Do not use *mad* for *angry* in formal situations, though both are standard, for *mad* implies "insane" to many people.

John was *angry* (not *mad*) because of the delay.

Most. Do not use the adjective *most* for the adverb *almost* (328); note also that *almost* modifies indefinite pronouns: *almost* everybody, *almost* anyone (316):

We sold *almost* (not *most*) all the tickets.

672 Nohow. This adverb has been incorrectly used so long to create double negative constructions that, though it is standard in sense, it is best not to use it at all.

This machine won't run *at all* (not *nohow*).

None. This word has long been accepted as singular or plural:

None *were* pleased with the result.

None of the girls *was* present.

Off—from. Do not misuse *off* or *off of* for *from:*

He bought the book *from* (not *off* or *off of*) me.

Off of. The *of* is superfluous; when used it is informal.

He jumped *off* (not *off of*) the car.

Party. Do not use for *person* except in terms of law or in a jocular sense.

I saw the *person* (not *party*) who won the prize.

Raise—rear. Raise is now in good standard usage for "bring up" without distinction of kind, but the following distinctions have been made up to now.

They *reared* three children.

He *raised* hogs for market.

Raise—rise. In its usual meanings *raise* is transitive and takes a receiver of its action; its principal parts are *raise—raised—raised*. *Rise* is intransitive and almost never takes an object; its principal parts are *rise—rose—risen* (217):

> Jim *raised* (not *rose*) the window.
>
> The plane *rose* (not *raised*) quickly as it flew away.

673   **Real.** Avoid using the adjective *real* for the adverbs *very* or *really* (311).

> She is *very* (not *real*) talented and *really* well educated.
>
> His boat was in *real* (actual) danger.

Reason. A statement containing *the reason is* is preferably completed by a *that* clause:

> The reason he succeeded is *that* (not *because*) he worked hard.

Reverend, Honorable. Do not place a surname immediately after either of these terms: *The Reverend George Smith, The Reverend Mr. Smith,* (not *Reverend Smith*); *The Honorable Susan Miller, The Honorable Mrs. Miller.*

Set—sit. *Set* is usually transitive and takes a receiver of its action; its principal parts are *set—set—set*. *Sit* is usually intransitive and does not take an object; its principal parts are *sit—sat—sat* (217):

> *Set* (not *sit*) the chair in the corner.
>
> We *sat* (not *set*) on the grass to rest.

So. Do not use it as an intensive in formal writing:

> He is *extremely* (not *so*) careful.

674   **Suspicion.** It is not in good use as a verb:

> They *suspected* (not *suspicioned*) him of theft.

This here—that there. Omit the dialectal *here* and *there*.

> I like *this* (not *this here*) model and not *that* (not *that there*) one.

To—at. Do not use *to* for *at* in such sentences as this:

> He is *at* (not *to*) home now.

Wait on. Do not use the dialectal *wait on* for *wait for*:

> Do not *wait for* (not *wait on*) me if my plane is late.

Way—ways. Use the singular form in sentences like this:

> He rode a short *way* (not *ways*) with us.

Widow woman. Omit *woman*:

> She is a *widow* (not *widow woman*).

Wire. Should not be used for *telegram* in formal writing:

> I will send you a *telegram* (not *wire*) tomorrow.

Without no. Do not use this double negative (336)

> He worked without *any* (not *no*) plans.

Pronunciation

675 The only sure guide to correct pronunciation is a standard dictionary. The words listed here are some of those about whose pronunciation many people are uncertain. The words with a number are recorded as having two or three acceptable pronunciations. Other faults lie in stressing the wrong syllable or by adding an extra one. In some instances, long and short vowel sounds are confused. It is best to learn one correct form and stick to it.

abdomen [2]	coupon [2]	grimace [2]	library
acclimate [2]	creek [2]	harass [2]	literature [5]
admirable	defect [2]	hearth	maintenance
adult [2]	despicable [2]	height	mischievous
almond [3]	detail [2]	heinous	museum
apparatus [2]	docile [2]	horizon	paraffin
apricot [2]	encore [3]	hospitable [2]	penalize [2]
architect	exquisite [2]	idea [3]	pergola [2]
athlete	finance [3]	impious [2]	pumpkin [2]
automobile [3]	forehead [4]	impotent	quantity
bouquet [2]	formidable [3]	industry	recognize
chauffeur [2]	gape [2]	inquiry [4]	research [2]
chic	garage [3]	interesting [3]	sagacious [2]
cognomen [2]	genuine	irreparable	salmon
column	gondola [2]	irrevocable	surprise
combatant [2]	government [2]	Italian [2]	sword [2]
comparable	granary [2]	laboratory [3]	vagary [5]
condolence [2]	gratis [2]	lamentable [2]	villain

Figures of Speech

676 A **figure of speech** is a variation from the ordinary method of expression for the sake of effect. Though there are many figures of speech, the two in most common use are the **simile** and the **metaphor**. Others are **personification, hyperbole, metonymy,** and **synecdoche**. Figures of speech are employed effectively in both prose and poetry. Good examples of the use of the simile may be found in such familiar poems as Shelley's "To a Skylark" and Kilmer's "Trees."

677 A **simile** is a direct comparison, introduced by *like* or *as*, of two things which in their general nature are different from each other:

She is *like a shining star*.   His hair is black *as* night.

678 A **metaphor** is implied comparison. Instead of stating the comparison, as in the simile, the likeness is suggested by terms not literally applicable to each other:

She is a *shining star*.   A *wave of emotion* overcame him.

679 Do not use mixed metaphors, such as these:

He is *aflame* with a *thirst* for knowledge.

Life is not all a rough *sea;* sometimes its *pathway* is smooth.

When a **simile** or a **metaphor** becomes involved and farfetched it is called a **conceit**.

680 **Personification** is the figure of speech in which some human characteristic is attributed to an inanimate thing:

The *friendly* hills seemed to *welcome* us.

681 **Hyperbole** is exaggeration for the purpose of emphasis and without any intention of being taken literally:

I am *completely starved.*

682 **Metonymy** is the substitution of the name of the whole for the name of the part, while **synecdoche** is the substitution of the part for the whole.

I am reading *Stevenson* (i.e., a book or poem by him).

This *camera* is broken (i.e., some part of it is broken).

They were stopped by a *badge* (i.e., a man with a badge, a policeman).

The ships dipped their *colors* (i.e., their flags).

Syllabication

683 Syllabication was originally a device of early printers to break words at the end of the printed line in order to give equal spacing between words and to keep the right margin aligned and parallel with the left margin. In general, the division in printed form follows the syllables of the spoken language. But, as there are so many exceptions due to the variations in the spelling and derivation of English words, the only sure guide to ascertain the correct current use is to refer to a good dictionary rather than to rely on one's ear.

EXAMPLE: syl-lab-i-ca-tion (spelled). si-lab-i-ca-tion (pronounced). The following rules should be followed in handwriting and typing:

1. Never divide words pronounced as one syllable: *drowned.*

2. Never divide words of two syllables with one a single vowel: *even, over.*

3. Do not divide the parts of a name: *John Smith, Mr. Jones.*

4. Do not divide numbers or abbreviations: 10,000, *C.O.D., SOS.*

5. Do not divide endings such as: *-tial, -tion, -cious, -geous.*

6. Do not separate a final syllable of one or two letters: *-a, -ed, -es.*

7. Do not divide hyphened compounds except at the hyphen: *all-around, all- around.*

Spelling—Words Often Confused

684 English, like other languages, has a number of paired words that cause confusion. There are four classes of such words.

1. **Homonyms.** These words are identical in spelling and pronunciation, but they differ in origin and meaning:

butter, food; *butter*, one who butts
pool, water; *pool*, the game

2. **Homophones.** These words are identical in pronunciation, but they differ in origin, spelling, and meaning:

fair, market; *fare*, food and drink; *fare*, tariff
red, color; *read*, past tense of *read*

3. **Homographs.** These words are identical in spelling, but they differ in origin, meaning, and sometimes in pronunciation:

fair, market; *fair*, beautiful
wind, air current; *wind*, to coil

4. **Heteronyms.** These words are identical in spelling, but they differ in origin, pronunciation, and meaning:

bass, fish; *bass*, male voice, musical term
row, a line; *row*, a fight

♦ Sometimes **homographs** that are in the pattern of *fair* in Number 3 are loosely classified as **homonyms.**

♦ Words such as "head" in English, "tête" in French, "cabeza" in Spanish, are true **synonyms** when used in their literal meaning—in these illustrations, anatomical.

Here are homophones which everyone should be able to spell and define correctly (in English there are at least three hundred seventy-five such paired word groups):

aisle—isle	beach—beech	canvas—canvass
all—awl	beat—beet	capital—capitol
altar—alter	beau—bow	ceiling—sealing
ant—aunt	been—bin	cell—sell
arc—ark	bell—belle	cellar—seller
ascent—assent	berth—birth	cent—sent—scent
ate—eight	bier—beer	cereal—serial
aught—ought	blew—blue	choir—quire
bail—bale	board—bored	chord—cord
bait—bate	born—borne	clause—claws
ball—bawl	bough—bow	coarse—course
bare—bear	brake—break	council—counsel
base—bass	buy—by	creak—creek
be—bee	calendar—calender	currant—current

dear—deer	lessen—lesson	rye—wry
dew—due	lie—lye	sail—sale
die—dye	load—lode	scene—seen
done—dun	loan—lone	sea—see
earn—urn	made—maid	seam—seem
fain—feign	mail—male	seine—sane
faint—feint	main—mane	sew—sow—so
fair—fare	manner—manor	shone—shown
feat—feet	mantel—mantle	sight—site—cite
fir—fur	meat—meet	slay—sleigh
flea—flee	medal—meddle	sleight—slight
flew—flue	might—mite	slew—slue—slough
flour—flower	miner—minor	soar—sore
fore—four	moan—mown	sole—soul
foul—fowl	muscle—mussel	some—sum
freeze—frieze	night—knight	son—sun
gait—gate	none—nun	staid—stayed
great—grate	one—won	stair—stare
groan—grown	pail—pale	stake—steak
guest—guessed	pain—pane	stationary—stationery
hair—hare	pause—paws	steal—steel
hale—hail	pair—pare—pear	stile—style
hall—haul	peace—piece	straight—strait
hart—heart	peal—peel	suite—sweet
heal—heel	plain—plane	tail—tale
hear—here	pore—pour	their—there
heard—herd	pray—prey	threw—through
heir—air	pride—pried	throne—thrown
hew—hue	principal—principle	to—too—two
hoes—hose	profit—prophet	toe—tow
hole—whole	rain—rein—reign	vail—veil—vale
holy—wholly	raise—raze	vain—vane—vein
hour—our	read—reed	vice—vise
idol—idle	read—red	wade—weighed
in—inn	real—reel	waist—waste
jam—jamb	rest—wrest	wait—weight
kernel—colonel	rhyme—rime	ware—wear
knead—need	right—write—wright—rite	warn—worn
knew—new	ring—wring	wave—waive
knot—not	road—rode—rowed	way—weigh
know—no	role—roll	week—weak
lain—lane	rose—rows	whole—hole
lead—led	rough—ruff	wood—would

Spelling

685 THE WRITTEN WORD   An essential characteristic of good writing is correct spelling. American English in its written form was initially

recorded in Samuel Johnson's first American dictionary published in New Haven, Connecticut, in 1798. This Samuel Johnson was not related to Doctor Samuel Johnson, the sage of Fleet Street, whose famous English dictionary was published in London in 1755.

In the American Johnson's work the beginnings of simplified spelling first appeared, later to be amplified in Noah Webster's *American Dictionary* of 1828. There is for the English language no authoritative arbiter of usage such as the *Académie Française* or the *Accademia della Crusa* of France and Italy "to sift the husks and purify the language." In general, dictionaries of the English language rely on recording the language as it is "used" rather than "how it ought to be." It is inevitable then that different dictionaries will reflect the tastes of different times, different places, and different lexicographers. Nevertheless, there is such a wide area of agreement in our standard American English spelling that a misspelled word is inexcusable.

Spelling List and Vocabulary Builder

The words in this list should be learned and mastered as they comprise a working vocabulary of high frequency and usefulness. Most of these words are among those frequently misspelled by writers and printers alike. At times, it is a matter of confusing words very similar in form: confid*ent* (adjective) and confid*ant* (noun). Again, such words as *elicit* and *illicit* are often used in error because of a partial similarity in sound. The suffixes *-able* and *-ible* are not always correctly distinguished.

The homophones, in section 684, are not repeated in this list. They should be added to the list as a genuine part of a good vocabulary. To illustrate, consider this EXAMPLE: An important spelling error may occur, when we permit the "advice" of *counsel* to "advise" us to speak out in the *council*, although we were ruled out of order by the council chairperson.

The principal parts of irregular verbs, in section 204, are to be considered as a part of this spelling list and should be learned for both their correct use and their spelling in writing. EXAMPLE: Now that I *know* him—and *knowing* him as well as I do—I *knew* that I should have *known* all about him before this.

The word list, in section 675, on developing dictionary skills, provides another group that includes forty-nine words not appearing in this section.

♦ Note that, in this listing, the dictionary style of entry for run-in words is used: thus, *agree, -able, -ment* is to be read as *agree, agreeable, agreement*. Note also that *-ing* or *-d, -ed,* is used to indicate an adjective formed on a noun or verb base rather than the participle, present or past form, or a part of a verb phrase (41, 181).

abattoir
abhor, –rence
abhorrent
ability
absence
absolute, –ly
absorb, –able,
    –ing
absorption
abundance
abundant, –ly
accede
accelerate, –ed
acceleration
accept, –ed,
    –ance
access, –ible
accident, –al,
    –ally
accommodate
accommodation
accompanist
accompany, –ing
accomplice
accomplish, –ed,
    –ment
accord, –ance
account, –ing
accumulate, –d
accurate, –ly
accustom, –ed
ache
achieve, –ment
acknowledge, –d
acknowledgment
acquaint, –ance
acquire, –d
across
actual, –ly
adapt, –able,
    –ability
addition, –al
address, –ed, –ee
admissible
admit, –tance
advantage, –ous
advertise, –d,
    –ment

advertising
advice
advise, –ment
aerial
aeronautics
affect, –ed, –ing
affection, –ate,
    –ately
affidavit
against
aggravate, –d
aggravation
aggressive, –ly
aghast
agree, –d, –able,
    –ment
agricultural
agriculture
alcohol, –ic
allow, –ed, –ance
all right
already
although
altogether
aluminum
always
amateur, –ish
ammonia
among
amount
amuse, –d,
    –ment
analogous
analysis
analyze
ancient, –ly
angle, –d
anniversary
announce, –d,
    –ment
annual, –ly
answer
antenna
anticipate, –d
anticipation
anxiety
anxious, –ly,
    –ness

apologize
apology
apparatus
apparent, –ly
appeal, –ed,
    –able, –ing
appear, –ance
appetite
application
apply
appoint, –ed,
    –ive
appreciate, –d
appreciative, –ly
approach, –ed,
    –able
approximate, –d,
appropriation
approval
approve, –d,
approximate, –d,
    –ly
aquanaut
arbitrary, –ly
arctic
argue
arguing
argument
arrange, –d,
    –ment
article
artificial
ascend, –able
ascendant
ascertain, –ed,
    –able
assassin, –ate,
    –ated
assiduous, –ly
assign, –ed, –able,
    –ment
assist, –ed, –ance
association
assume, –d
assurance
astronaut
athlete

athletic
attach, –ed, –able
attack, –ed, –able
attempt, –ed
attend, –ed,
    –ance
attention
attitude
attorney
attract, –ed, –ive,
    –ively
audience
authoritative, –ly
authority
automobile
autumn, –al
auxiliary
avail, –able, –ing
average, –d
aviation
awful, –ly
awkward, –ly
backslide
baggage
balance, –d
ballet
ballistics
balloon
ballot
bandage, –d
banquet
banquette
bargain, –ed
barrel, –led
base, –ment
basis
battalion
becoming, –ly
beggar, –ed
beginning
behavior, –al
belief
believe, –r
belligerent, –ly
beneficent
beneficial, –ly
beneficiary
benefit, –ed

bicycle, –d
biscuit
blizzard
bookkeeping
boundary
breadth
breath
breathe, –d
brief, –ly
brilliant, –ly
broad, –ly
bruise, –d
budget, –ed
bulletin
buoyant, –ly
bureau, –crat
burglar, –ize
bury
business, –like
busy, –ness
cabin
cafeteria
campaign, –er
cancel, –ed
candidate
canoe
capacity
captain
career
careless, –ness
carriage
carrier
carry, –ing
cashier, –d
categorical, –ly
category
caution, –ed,
    –ary
celebrate, –d
celebration
cemetery
century
certain, –ly
certificate
certification
changeable
character, –ize
chauffeur

chemistry
chief, –tain
chocolate
choice
choose
chose, –n
circular, –ize
civilization
climate
climb, –ed
clothe, –s
clothing
coach, –ed
coalesce, –d
coherent, –ly
collar
college
collegiate
color, –ful
colossus
column
coming
commence
commercial, –ly
commission, –ed,
    –er
committee, –man,
    –woman
communicate, –d
community
comparative, –ly
comparison
compel, –led
competent, –ly
competition
complain
complement,
    –ary
complexion, –ed
compliment, –ed,
    –ary
computer, –ize
concede, –d
conceive, –d
concern, –ed,
    –ing
concert, –ed
concession

conclude, –d
concrete, –ly
condemn, –ed
condition, –ed,
   –al
confection, –er,
   –ery
confer, –red,
   –ring
conference
confidant
confidence
confident, –ial,
   –ly
congratulate
congratulation
connoisseur
consensus
conscience
conscientious
consequence
consequent, –ial
considerable
considerably
consistent, –ly
constitution, –al
contempt, –ible
continual, –ly
continue, –d
control, –led,
   –ling, –lable
controversial
convenient
convenience
convince, –d
cool, –ly
co-op
cooperate, –d
cordial, –ly
corduroy
corespondent
corporation
correspond, –ed,
   –ent, –ence
cough
couldn't
country
county

courage, –ous
courteous, –ly
courtesy
cousin
couth
critic, –ism
cruel, –ly
curiosity
curriculum
curtain
custom, –er
   –ary
cylinder
daily
decease, –d
deceive, –d
decide
decision
decisive
declaration
decorate, –d
decorative
defense
defensive
definite, –ly
definition
definitive, –ly
delicious, –ly
delirious
depend, –ant,
   –ent, –ency
depot
descend, –ed,
   –ant, –ent
describe, –d
description
descriptive, –ly
desert, –ed
deserts
deserve, –d
design, –ing
desirous
desperate, –ly
dessert
determine, –d
develop, –ed,
   –ment
diamond

dictionary
didn't
difference
different, –ly
difficult, –y
dilapidated
diminish, –ed
diphtheria
diploma
diplomat
direct, –ly, –or
disagree, –able,
   –ment
disappear, –ance,
   –ed
disappoint, –ed,
   –ment
disapprove, –d
disaster
disastrous, –ly
discipline, –d
discover, –ed,
   –able
discuss, –ed,
   –ion, –ible
disease, –d
dissipate, –d
distinguish, –ed,
   –able
distribute, –d
distribution
divide, –d
divine
divisible
division, –al
doctor
dominant
don't
doubt, –ed
dual
duchess
duel
duly
duplicate, –d
duplication
during
dyeing
dying

earnest, –ly,
  –ness
easily
easy
economic, –s, –al
economy
ecstacy
effect, –ive, –ual
effervescent
efficiency
efficient, –ly
eighth
either
elaborate, –d,
  –ly, –ness
electric, –ity, –al
electronic, –s
elephant
elevator
elicit, –ed
eligible
eliminate, –d
embarrass, –ing,
  –ment
emerge, –d, –ncy
emphasis
emphasize, –d
employ, –ed, –er,
  –ee, –able,
  –ment
encourage, –d,
  –ment
encyclopedia
endeavor
endorse, –ment
enemy
engineer, –ing
enormous, –ly
enough
entertain, –ed,
  –er, –ment
enthusiast, –ic
entrance
envelope
envelopment
environment, –al
equip, –ped,
  –ment

equivalence
equivalent
ere, e're
especially
essential, –ly
establish, –ed,
  –ment
every
evidence
exaggerate, –d
exaggeration
exceed, –ed
excellent, –ly
excellence
except, –ed
  –able, –ion,
  –ing
excess, –ive,
  –ively
excite, –d, –dly,
  –ment
executive
exercise, –d
exhibit, –ed,
  –ion
exhilarating
exhort, –ation
existence
existent
exorbitant, –ly
expedition, –ary
expensive, –ly
experience, –d
explain, –ed
explanation
explicit, –ly
express, –ed, –ly,
  –ion
expressive, –ness
exquisite, –ly
extend, –ed, –ible
extension
extinct, –ion
extreme, –ly
facilitate, –d
fallacy
familiar
famous, –ly

fascinate, –d
fascinating
fashion, –ed,
  –able
fatigue, –d
fatiguing
faucet
favorite
feature, –d
February
federal
fertile
fictitious
field
fierce
fiery (fire)
filth, –y, –iness
final, –ly
finance
financial, –ly
flight
flourish, –ing
foreign, –er
foreword
formally
formerly
fortunate, –ly
forty
forward
fountain, –head
fourth
freight
friend, –ly,
  –liness
fulfill, –ed,
  –ment
fundamental, –ly
gage
garage
gardener
gasoline
gauge
general, –ly
generosity
generous, –ness
genius
genuine, –ly,
  –ness

geographic, –al
geography
ghastly
glorious, –ly
government, –al
governor
gracious, –ly
gradation
graduation
grammar
grandeur
grateful, –ly
gratitude
grease
great, –ly
grief
grievous, –ly
grocery
guarantee, –d
guard, –ed
guardian, –ship
guide, –d
guilt, –y, –ily,
   –inesss
guttural, –ly
gymnasium
hammer, –ed
handkerchief
handle, –d
handsome, –ly
hansom (cab)
happen, –ing
happiness
harass, –ment
harbor
hardiness
hardness
haste
hastily
height
heretofore
herringbone
hesitate
hesitation
heyday
hinder, –ing
hindrance
Hippocratic
   (oath)

historic, –al
history
holiday
honor, –ed,
   –able
horrible, –ness
horrid, –ly, –ness
hospitable
hospital, –ity,
   –ize,
   –ization
human, –e
humor, –less,
   –ous
hundred
hundredth
hungry
hurricane
hydrogen
hymn, –al
hypercritical
hypocrisy
hypocrite
hypocritical
idea
identified
identify
identity
ignorance
illiteracy
illiterate
illustrate, –d
illustration
imagination
imagined
imitation
immediate, –ly
immense, –ly
immortal, –ity
impatience
impatient, –ly
impedance
import, –ed, –ant,
   –antly,
   –ance,
   –ation
impossible
impresario

improve, –d,
   –ment
incessant, –ly
incidence
incident, –s, –al,
   –ally
incompatibility
incompatible
inconvenience
inconvenient, –ly
incorrigible
incredible
independent, –ly
indict, –ment
indispensable
individual, –ly
industrial
industrious, –ness
inevitable, –ness
inferior, –ity
influence
influential
ingenous
ingenuous
inimitable
innocent
innocuous
inoculate
inoculation
instance, –d
instant, –aneous,
   –ly
instead
institute
institution, –al
insurance
intelligence
intelligent, –ly
interest, –ing,
   –ingly
interfere, –nce
interpret, –ation
interrupt, –ed, –er
interview, –er,
   –ed, –ing
intimate, –ly
invalid

invalid, –ate,
   –ated
invariably
investigate, –d
investigation
invitation
invite, –d
invoice
irrelevant
irreparable
irresistible
irrigate
irrigation
island
issue, –d
jackknife
jaguar
janitor
jargon
jaundice, –d
jealous, –y
jewelry
journal, –ism
journey
judgment
juicy
justice
kitchen
khaki
kindergarten
knickknack
knowledgeable
knowledge
label, –ed
laboratory
language
later
latter
laugh
laundry
lawyer
league
lecture
leeway
legal, –ity, –ize
legislate
legislature
leisure, –ly

length
lettuce
liability
liable
librarian
library
license, –d
lieutenant
lighten, –ing, –ed
lightning
likely
linoleum
liquefy
liquefiable
liquid, –ate,
   –ation
liquor
listen, –er, –able
literary
literate
literature
liveliest
livelihood
lively
living
lodgment
loneliness
lonely
loose, –ly, –ned
lose, –r
losing
lovable
love, –ly, –liness
lunch, –eon
machine, –d
magazine
magnificent, –ly
maintain
maintenance
majority
mammoth
manage, –able
   –ment
manifold
manufactory
manufacture, –d,
   –r
manyfold

marriage
marry, –ing
material, –ly
matériel
maternity
mathematics
mattress
mayor, –alty
measure, –d
medicinal
medicine
medium
mercenary
merchandise
merchantman
merit, –ed
message
metal, –lic
mettle, –some
mileage
millionaire
miniature
minimum
minute
mirror, –ed
miscellaneous
mischief
mischievous
miser, –ly
miserable
misery
missionary
missile
misspell, –ed
   –ing
moccasin
moist, –ure,
   –urize
momentous
monument, –al
moral, –ly
morale
mortgage, –d
mountainous
murmur, –s
musician, –ly
mutilate, –d
myth, –ical

mythology
nadir
naphtha
narrate
narrative
natural, –ly
nautical
naval
navel
navigating
navigation, –al
necessary
necessity
nickel
niece
nihilism
nineteen, –th
ninetieth
ninety
nonsense
notice, –able
notwithstanding
nowadays
nuclear
nuisance
obbligato
obdurate
occasion
occur, –red,
   –rence
octopus
oculist
ominous, –ly
omission
omit, –ted
onerous
operate
operating
opinion, –ated
opportunity
opposite
opposition
oppress, –ed, –ive,
   –or
optician
optimism
optimistic
oratorio
oratory

orchestra, –l
origin, –al, –ality
oxygen
pamphlet
paragraph
parallel, –ism
paralysis
paralyze
paraphernalia
parenthesis
parliament, –ary
participial
participle
particular, –ize,
   –ly
passed
pastime
pastor
paternity
pavilion
peasant
peculiar, –ly
penance
pendulum
penguin
peninsula, –r
penitent, –ial,
   –iary
perforation
perform, –ance
perhaps
permanent, –ly
permissible
permissive, –ness
perseverance
persist, –ent,
   –ence
person, –al, –able,
   –ality, –alty
personnel
perspiration
persuade, –r
persuasion
pertain, –ing
pervade
phenomenal, –ly
Philippines
philosophic, –al
philosophy

physical
physician
physicist
physics
picnic, –king
plain, –ly
plan, –ned
plane
plaque
plastic, –s
pleasant, –ly,
   –ness
pneumonia
poison, –er, –ous
ponderous, –ly
possession
possibility
possible
practical, –ly, –ity
practice
precede, –nce
precious
prefer, –red,
   –ence,
   –ential
preform, –ed
prejudice, –d
preparation
prepare
preservation
preserve, –d
prevalent, –ly
preventive
prison, –er
privilege, –d
probable
probably
procedure
proceed, –ing, –s
profess, –or
proffer, –ed
prominent
promontory
pronounce, –d
pronunciation
propel, –ler
prophecy
prophesy
psychiatry

psychology
pumpkin
pursue, –r
pursuit
quaking
qualified
qualify
quandary
quarantine
quarrel
quarter, –ed
questionnaire
quiescent
quiet, –ed, –ly
quite
quorum
quote
quoth
radar
radiant, –ly
radiation
radiator
real, –ly
realize
rebut, –tal
recede
receipt, –ed
receive, –d
receptacle
reciprocal, –ly
reclaim, –ed
reclamation
recognition
recognize, –d
recommend, –ed,
    –ation
redundant
refer, –red, –ence
refrigerator
rehabilitation
relevance
relevant, –ly
relieve
religious, –ly
reluctance
reluctant, –ly
remembrance
renegade
reparation

repetition
represent, –ation,
    –ative
rescind
reservoir
respect, –ed, –ful,
    –fully
responsibility
restaurant
rheumatism
rhythm, –ic, –ical
ridiculous, –ly
roommate
rummage
sabbath
sacrament
sacrifice
sacrilegious
sagacious
sail, –ing, –er, –or
salary
sandwich
sanitary
satellite
satire
satisfaction
satisfactory
scarcity
schedule, –d
science
scientific
scissors
secretary
seize, –d
seminary
separate, –d, –ly
sergeant
several, –ly
shepherd, –ess
shining
shoulder, –s
shrubbery
siege
significant, –ly
silhouette
similar, –ly
simultaneous, –ly
since
sincere, –ly

ski, –ing
slimmest
sociable
social
solemn, –ity
sophomore
source
sovereign, –ty
spaceship
sparsely
specie
species
specific
specimen
speech
sphere
statue
stature
statute
straight, –en
straitjacket
stratagem
strategy
strenuous, –ly
stretch, –able,
    –ability
stubborn, –ness
studying
subtle
suburban
succeed, –ing
success, –ive,
    –ively
sufficient, –ly
suffrage
sugar
suit, –able,
    –ability
summary
superficial, –ly
superintend, –ent
supersede
suppress, –ed,
    –ion
surprise, –d
surround, –ed,
    –ing
syllable
symmetrical

symmetry
synonym, –ous
system, –atic,
    –atically
tacit
tariff
technical, –ly
technique
telegram
temperament
temperature
temporarily
temporary
tend, –ency
terrible
territorial
territory
theater
theatrical, –ly
therefore
they, –'re
thief
thievery
thorough, –ly,
    –ness
though
thousandths
tire, –d, –less,
    –dness
tobacco
tobogganing
together
tongue
topography
tortuous
torturous
touch, –ing, –able
tragedy

tranquil, –lity
transfer, –red,
    –rence
transistor, –ize
treasure, –d, –r
truculent
true, –ness
truly
truth
tying
typical, –ly
typography
tyrannical, –ly
unanimous, –ly
undoubted, –ly
universal, –ly
university
unmistakable
unnecessary
upper, –most
use, –d, –ful, –less
usual, –ly
usurious
utter, –ance
vacation
vaccination
vacillate
vacillation
valuable
variety
various
vegetable
vehicle
velocity
vengeance
vertical, –ly
vicinity
victuals

view, –ing
vilify
villain
visible
visit, –or, –ation
vitamin, –s
vocation
voice, –d
volume
voluble
waggish
wander, –ing,
    –lust
warrant, –ee, or,
    –y
weather, –ed
Wednesday
weight
weird, –ness
whether
which
whom
whose
width
witch
withhold
won't
worst
wouldn't
writing
yacht
yearn
yeoman
yield
you're
zeal, –ous, –ously
zenith

686 **The Dictionary as a Tool**   One of the areas of difference in usage is, of course, the spelling of the words and forms of the written language. The young writer will find that the best tool for controlling this aspect of expression is the dictionary. Its constant use is a *must*. The dictionary verifies one's spelling when there is doubt; where more than one form is acceptable, it records them in one place; when certain spellings have restricted application, it states the fact; and when regional differences affect the choice of form (American vs. British, standard vs. dialectal, serious vs. humorous, for example), the dictionary indicates the preference.

Compounding

687 English compound words give much spelling trouble to writers everywhere, because there are so many of them. Here is an area where the "rules" applicable are often at variance with actual usage. Memorize as many as you can. In fact, several books detailing the technique have been written about the compounding of English words. Note these few illustrative examples—of the large number of patterns possible:

airplane	= noun + noun
press agent	= noun (used as adjective) + noun
spoilsport	= verb + noun
good-looking	= adjective + participle
uptown	= adverb + noun
newlywed	= adverb + participle
newly wed couple	= adverb + participle + noun
old-age pension	= adjective + noun + noun
Mexican-American	= proper adjective + proper adjective

What is an English compound word? It is the combination of several standard words which, when used together, create a new concept of meaning. Thus, every *black bird* is not necessarily a *blackbird*; a *workingman* does not mean a *man* is *working*; a *storeroom* does not mean a *room* in a *store*; a *cornflower* is not the *flower* of the *corn* plant. Each compound, then, becomes a word in its own right.

There are three types of compounds to be considered and one of these (3) is not technically a compound: (1) The solid form, *outlaw, textbook,* (to) *shortchange* (solideme); (2) the hyphenated form, *X-Ray, city-state, well-known* (hypheme); (3) the word-phrase form of two or more words, *red tape, printing press, post office, one hundred and one* (men), *three week's* (pay). Your dictionary is the proper source for determining what is the actual and correct form to be used in writing. Once you have chosen the correct form, always be consistent in using it.

688 THE UNIT MODIFIER This hyphened form is a conventional, recorded two-noun phrase or an improvised literal compound adjective which is used only before a noun:

cast iron   – a *cast-iron* bridge
gas meter – a *gas-meter* reading
folk dance – a *folk-dance* festival
rush hour – a *rush-hour* crush
air mail   – an *air-mail* letter
               – an *ever-winding* road
               – an *always-smoking* chimney
               – a *reddish-brown* paint
               – an *off-and-on* game
               – a *tongue-in-cheek* remark

About Words

689 FOREIGN WORDS AND PHRASES This class of words must be carefully checked as to spelling, including accent marks, and as to whether they are or are not considered anglicized; that is, whether they should be italicized or not as foreign words or phrases:

auf Wiedersehn	– German
au fait	– French
amuck	– Malayan: *amock*
Calvary	– Late Latin: *Calvaria*
Cordoba	– Spanish: *Cordova*
Van Gogh [van go]	– Dutch: *vän Khokh*
habeas corpus	– English Law Latin (1679)

690 MISSPELLING AS AN "ART FORM."

The Duk iz a kind ov short legged hen.
They kan sale on the water as natral and eazy as a grease spot.
Duks hav a broad bill which enables them tew eat their food without anny spoon.
There aint any room on the outside of a Duk for enny more feathers.
The duk don't kro like a rooster, but quaks like a duk.
                                        —JOSH BILLINGS (Henry W. Shaw) 1818–1885

691 VOCABULARY The ability to express one's thoughts and to understand the expression of the thoughts of others can be measured by one's knowledge of the meaning of words. A good and expressive vocabulary is, obviously, an invaluable aid to success in any field. It must include the words in the vocabularies of the student's special fields of interest—be it art, music, engineering, agriculture, space science, or ecology—with their **synonyms** (words of the same general meaning but different in their specific application) and **antonyms** (words of opposite meaning).

692 THE USE OF THE DICTIONARY The use of a standard unabridged dictionary is valuable in building a vocabulary. It gives extensive information about every word—pronunciation, part of speech (38), derivation, illustrations of current usage, various meanings, synonyms, and antonyms. In a section, usually at the front of the dictionary, all the symbols used in its pronunciation system are explained, and the diacritical marks are fully illustrated.

693 A PLAN FOR VOCABULARY BUILDING To develop a good, working vocabulary requires time, patience, and persistence. One good plan is to write in a notebook all unfamiliar words that one reads or hears. Unfamiliar words and word uses found in reading one's own books should be marked so that the meaning may be studied in context (696). A periodic review of what has been noted reinforces learning.

694 VOCABULARY AND VERSE Through the writing of rhymed verse (564–568), one may enlarge one's vocabulary, because words must be selected for meaning as well as for sound. The sonnet (573, 574) is a good stanza form to use because of its rigid rhyme requirements. The limerick (576) is also a good form, which may be used in either light or serious mood. Writing parodies (imitations) of popular verse is not only fun but also a profitable exercise in word substitution. Specimens of these types of writing are to be found in current newspapers and magazines. The improvised limerick and sonnet below suggest possibilities:

SUCCESS

You think you are well on your way,
Assured you make progress each day;
Yet, nevertheless,
Your final success
Depends on the words that you say.

WORDS

The words we use may be but stumbling blocks
To make more arduous our upward way—
Along our path but rough, projecting rocks
To bruise our weary feet from day to day;
And yet, it's folly we are thus oppressed,
For words may help us on to higher things:
One who with mastery of words is blest
Not only upward toils, but starward goes on wings.
Unwise are they who fail to count the cost
Of clumsy, careless words that flout success,
But wisdom theirs who see as won or lost
Through use of words life's greatest happiness.
He who for artistry in language strives
Finds rich return: with words we shape our lives.

695 SPECIAL-SUBJECT DICTIONARIES AND GLOSSARIES Almost every area of knowledge today has its own special vocabulary of words and terms. Sometimes they are included as a part of a book on a given subject to show how the author has used them in developing the subject. At times the use may differ, in some limiting aspect, from the standard definition of a word or phrase. A compilation of such word-usage is called a glossary. It may be included within a book as an appendix, or it may be extensive enough to be issued as a separate book or pamphlet.

In vocabulary building, such dictionaries and glossaries should not be overlooked, for they are a rich source of specialized information.

696 WORDS IN CONTEXT Context may be simply defined as the "weaving together of words." More formally it is described as "any phrase, sentence, or passage so closely connected to a word or words as to affect their meaning." (*Standard College Dictionary.*)

Thus the association of words with each other is important in vocabulary building. To illustrate, consider the word *eye*, the organ of vision in animals. By various figures of speech we have: a *black* eye (area); *brown* eye (color of the iris of the eye); keep an *eye* on (watch carefully); cast an *eye* over (look at); in the public *eye* (in the presence of); an evil *eye* (particular expression of); an *eye* for girls (interest in); the *eye* of the riot (focal point); the *eye* of the storm (central area); electric *eye* (in resemblance to the human eye); *eye* of the wind (direction); *eye* to *eye* (in agreement with).

Using the Library

697 THE LIBRARY Many libraries now use the Dewey Decimal System or the Library of Congress classification system. The Dewey system classifies all works exclusive of fiction into ten major groups and each group further into ten subgroups. Following is a simple description of the major groups:

000–099	General works, such as encyclopedias
100–199	Philosophy, psychology
200–299	Religion, mythology
300–399	Social sciences, such as government, sociology, economics, and books on clubs, holidays, and etiquette
400–499	Languages: grammar, linguistics
500–599	Pure science: mathematics, physics, chemistry, botany, zoology, earth science, biological sciences

600–699 Applied science: inventions, gardening, cooking, sewing, aeronautics, engineering, medicine, agriculture

700–799 Arts and recreation: such as drawing, painting, and music

800–899 Literature (except fiction)

900–999 History: travel, geography, biography

Certain books may not be shelved according to their class number.

1. Short-story collections may be marked SC and shelved separately. They are arranged alphabetically by the last name of the editor.

2. Books of biography are shelved according to the last name of the person they are about. Some libraries use the Dewey Decimal number 921, many prefer 92, and some use only the letter B to indicate biography. Below either 921, 92, or B on the catalogue card is the initial of the person written about.

3. Reference books like encyclopedias and atlases are usually shelved together. The letter R above the number indicates a reference book.

More precise in its ability to classify books is the Library of Congress classification system, in which a set of capital letters is combined with numbers. A broad area, such as literature, is indicated by a letter. A subdivision of that area is shown by a second capital letter, and further subdivisions are shown by numbers.

8

Structural Linguistics and Transformational/ Generative Grammars

During the Middle Ages in Europe—the period from 500 to 1500 A.D.— Latin was a truly international language. It was used by the literate people (scholars, clergy, nobles, etc.) to communicate with each other both at home and abroad. The speech of the uneducated people was in what we now call the vernacular (i.e., English, French, Italian, etc.).

Grammar, in those days, meant the study of literature, whether it was of a religious or secular nature—the same meaning it had for the Roman and Greek writers of antiquity. Hence the only grammar taught in the schools then was Latin grammar as an aid to the learning of Latin as a second language in both its oral and written form.

In 1362, William Langland, in his poem "The Vision of William Concerning Piers Plowman," gives us the earliest known reference in English to the word *grammar* ("gramer for gurles [girls], I gon furste to write"). And in 1605, Francis Bacon wrote in *On the Advancement of Learning* "concerning speech and words the consideration of them had produced the science of grammar."

By the middle of the 18th Century, grammar came to be considered as comprising *phonology* (the sound system of a language), *accidence* (the inflexional forms of a language and their proper combinations), and *syntax* (the structure of the sentences of a language). Today, we use the terms *morphology* (the study and description of the word formations of a language, including inflection, derivation, and compounding) and *syntax*.

The new systems of grammar studied in this unit clearly show that the "science of grammar" in recent times has been expanded to deal not only with questions about the functioning of a language but also with the phenomenon of language itself.

Structural Linguistics

698 Structural linguistics is a valuable method of studying language, especially a variety of languages, to determine how structure contributes to the semantic or lexical meaning of their vocabularies. It is perhaps particularly useful in analyzing the anything-but-primitive languages of tribal societies and in describing any spoken language, since it inter-relates its sounds, voice inflections, pauses, and other special features.

699 The traditional terminology of English grammar has had to be re-interpreted in modern times to apply more accurately to English. It was developed in the eighteenth century on terminology that originally applied to Greek and Latin grammars (*c.* 200 B.C. to *c.* A.D. 600), and English does not fit readily into such a mold. In the same way, the terminology that has been adapted to English must be further reconsidered if it is to fit other, quite different languages. Our "parts of speech," for example, are not the same as Navajo "parts of speech." Some languages have categories wholly lacking in English—forms for "things in sight" and "things not in sight," and the "aspects" of the Russian verb, are examples. For this reason a study of language based on structure—divorced as far as possible from the meaning of ordinary grammatical terminology—avoids some of the confusions and misconceptions that arise when terminology applied to one language is used for another.

700 Structural linguistics also offers valuable insights into our language to those who are thoroughly trained in traditional grammar. Those who undertake any advanced study of English must expect to become familiar with the terminology and approach of this relatively new method of language study.

701 OBJECTIVES OF GRAMMAR STUDY   It should be kept in mind, in studying a new approach to the explanation of a language, that the language itself is not changed because the description of it changes: the problems remain the same. Whatever system one studies, it should be one that can be applied to the problems of writing and speaking with clarity, with effectiveness, and with a minimum of irrelevant and unintended social friction. The problems of usage remain the same whatever the system of grammar, and (although there is room for difference of opinion) substantially the same answers should be given

to such questions as those concerning agreement of verbs, agreement of pronouns, the use of the subjunctive, the formation of plurals, capitalization, punctuation, and the other mechanics of writing. In other words, the rules may be reformulated but not changed (unless the usage changes) because the rules must reflect the usage of the society rather than the predilections of the grammarians. The objectives also should remain the practical ones of making more effective the use and comprehension of language in its spoken and written forms.

702 The **definitions** of structural linguistics are quite different from those of traditional grammar. No definitions yet developed are entirely free of ambiguities and unexplained terms. The structural linguist tries to avoid the problems of traditional definitions by defining his terms by means of structural examples and formal characteristics. To be complete, such definitions may involve so many formulas as to appear unwieldy. But, as with traditional definitions, sufficiently clear ideas can be given to permit further development by the use of additional examples and analogies. The following explanations are intended merely to give some idea of the approach used by some widely studied linguists. Since no two structural linguists as yet use quite the same terminology and definitions, those noted here certainly cannot be considered final or complete. This description is based primarily on the work of those who have tried to adapt the subject to undergraduate college students and even to high-school students, and it should be understood to be only a description in part of the technique employed.

703 The **parts of speech** in structural linguistics parallel in many ways those of traditional grammar, but there are important differences, as will be seen below. For this reason some linguists prefer to avoid traditional terms altogether, but since this introduction is intended for those already grounded in traditional terminology, it is obvious that parallels may be drawn and differences brought out. Many linguists do use the traditional terms **nouns** and **pronouns, verbs, adjectives,** and **adverbs** for the important form classes (forms showing recognizable phonetic or grammatical similarity), and these terms are used in this discussion.

Form Classes

704 The form class **nouns** and **pronouns** is illustrated by the italicized words as used in the patterns below:

The *boy* is honest.
The *boys* are honest.
The *boys* saw *him*.
He saw the *boys*.
They ate the *peaches*.

Words that fit into sentence positions structurally similar to those shown above are nouns or pronouns. These are not substitution patterns: one does not say "The *desk* is honest," "They ate the *courage*," though *desk* and *courage* are nouns. One must learn to recognize what patterns of words are structurally similar. The position of a word in a sentence helps to classify it, but one must understand sentence structure before words can be analyzed in this way. This knowledge applies to the study of all of the form classes.

705 One must also keep in mind that a large proportion of English words may be used as more than one part of speech (52). A toy boat may *sink* (verb) in a *sink* (noun). You may fall *down* (adverb) and not make a first *down* (noun) in a football game. One can determine the class of a word only when it is used in a sentence, but other tests may be also needed to determine the class of a word in a sentence (see 708).

706 Nouns and pronouns generally show **singular** and **plural number.** Those in this form class that correspond to nouns (53–61) usually add *s* to show the plural (see 76–93); those that correspond to pronouns (128) show number by entirely different words: *he* (*she*)—*they*; while the determiners (717) *this* and *that* have the plural forms *these* and *those.* Verbs (709) indicate a singular meaning in the third person present tense by adding *s*: He *runs*; they *run.*

707 Another **formal characteristic** of nouns—though not of pronouns—is that they may have another *s* ending (in writing marked by an apostrophe) to show possession or some such relationship (see 116–127). There are exceptions as explained in 121–122. Other characteristics of this class are that nouns and pronouns may be marked (or modified) by determiners (717) or adjectives (711) that are not in noun positions. Nouns and pronouns may also be marked in a different way (not modified) by prepositions (717). Nouns also correlate in many ways with pronouns. There are other characteristics that mark words of this form class, but these will illustrate what is meant by the formal and structural approach. "Mark" or "marker," in this context, means to point out by the form used or to predict, by its position in the structure, the form that normally follows.

708 Most nouns may be used to modify other nouns. For instance in the sentence "He planted a rose bush," *rose* is a noun, not an adjective (711), because it cannot be modified by an intensive (717), and so on, as adjectives are, and it cannot appear in other adjective positions. We do not say "it is a very rose bush" or "the bush is rose." (On the same basis traditional grammarians agree that there are eight categories for nouns used as adjectival modifers of other nouns to indicate concepts, such as "made of," "pertaining to," "characterized by," etc.)

709 The form class **verbs** is illustrated by the italicized words as used in the following patterns:

They *see* the fire.

He *came* alone.

Most verbs show some changes in form that are associated with tense (190), person (69), and number (see 170–215). Most of them regularly form definite patterns with auxiliaries (717) such as *may, can, is, was, had, have, should*. They usually have a form ending in *-ing* (attached to a basic form). It is quite common to consider the word *be* (*be, am, is, are, was, were, been, being*) as having a separate class of its own, and not as a form class verb even though it may also be used as an auxiliary verb.

710 Verbs may modify nouns: *singing* teakettle, *running* brook, *treated* leather. But some *-ing* and *-ed* words are adjectives (711)—those, for instance, that form a pattern with *very*: *interesting* person (He is *very interesting*). Also some *-ing* words may take noun positions: "His *writing* is very poor." (Compare 200–201.)

711 The form class **adjectives** is illustrated by the italicized words as used in the following patterns:

The boy was *good*.

The *slender* girl came in.

The very *efficient* secretary resigned.

Most adjectives have forms that show comparison (295).

712 The form class **adverbs** is illustrated by the italicized words as used in the following patterns:

He sang *beautifully*.

She *often* fails to meet the payments.

The dog jumped *up*.

Most adverbs also show comparison (327).

713 The **form classes** must be recognized if one is to understand a sentence; otherwise the sentence is ambiguous. The form of a word, as well as its position in the sentence, often indicates its form class. For example, many nouns end in *-tion, -ness* (*relation, goodness*); many verbs end in *-ing, -ed* (*bringing, acted*), but these endings sometimes also mark adjectives (710); many adjectives end in *-like, -ful, -less, -ish, -ous* (*childlike, graceful, fruitless, bookish, famous*); and many (not all) adverbs end in *-ly* (*prettily, slowly*), but some adjectives also end in *-ly* (*lovely, ugly, homely*).

714 While **formal characteristics** of words are of help in determining the form class to which a word belongs, they cannot be relied on fully. Distinctive forms are relatively rare in English, and formal characteristics may at times be completely at variance with structural considerations. For example, in the sentence "The richest lived on the north shore," the word *richest* has a formal characteristic of an adjective: the ending *-est*. It may also be modified, as are adjectives, by an intensive: the *very richest*. On the other hand, it is marked by *the* as a noun, it is tied like a noun to a verb, and it can otherwise be substituted for nouns in noun positions.

Frequently the view is taken that the position supersedes the form of the word and that therefore *richest* is a noun in the sentence given (Compare 316.)

Structure Words

715 **Structure words** require a large number of groups to be clearly distinguished. These words have little meaning of their own, but they contribute significantly to the structural meaning of sentences. Every linguist uses a different grouping of words, so all that can be done here is to illustrate the approach used by certain widely known linguists. This class of words is identified by some writers as "function words."

716 Structure-word groups include all words that are not included in the four form classes. They will of course include words traditionally called **prepositions, conjunctions,** or **interjections.** But they also include some words traditionally called **adjectives, adverbs,** or **verbs.** These groups include only a small number of English words—a few hundred. The form classes, of course, include hundreds of thousands of words.

717 An illustrative classification of structure-word groups:

Determiners: *a, an, the,* and sometimes *some, these, each,* and so on. These mark nouns.

Auxiliaries: *am, are, is, (be), may, will, should,* etc., when used with verbs. (The word *be* may also be a special form of verb.) Auxiliaries are verb markers.

Prepositions: *with, at, on, under,* etc. These words combine in patterns with nouns and pronouns.

Intensives (intensifers): words that generally lend emphasis to adjectives or adverbs (sometimes also to verbs): *very, really, rather, too,* etc. Unlike adverbs, some of these words do not pattern with verbs—one does not say, "He plays *very.*"

Coordinators: *and, but, or, nor, for,* etc. Only coordinating conjunctions are included. The sentence connectors, such as *therefore, however, nevertheless,* may be given a different designation.

Subordinators: words like *because, since, after* (subordinating conjunctions) that join sentence groups into larger structures. Words like *who, what, which* (relatives) are sometimes classified with this group, sometimes as a separate group.

Question markers: *who, where, what, which, how, why,* etc., when they signal a question.

There are other words like *yes, no, not, please, hello, good-by, oh,* and so on, that, to be accurately classified, would require a large number of group designations.

Phonemes

718 Speech is made up of a number of distinctive sound groups, called phonemes, that may be represented by symbols. Each phoneme has variations depending on its phonetic environment, but it is recognized by a native speaker as essentially the same sound wherever it occurs in the language. For example, the sound represented by *t* in English is not the same in any of the following words—*tone, stove, trip, butter, butler, eighth*—though it is the same phoneme. Stress, pitch, and juncture are also phonemes (720–723). An understanding of phonemes is requisite to the thorough study of foreign languages as well as of our own spoken language.

Morphemes

719 Any voice signal, phoneme, or group of phonemes that contributes to meaning and that recurs with a relatively constant meaning in different contexts is a **morpheme**—it cannot be further divisible into smaller meaningful elements. The word *girlish* is composed of the two morphemes *girl* and *-ish*; neither can be divided into smaller units which recur with the same meaning, but they both occur in other contexts with relatively the same meanings: that is, the morpheme *girl* has the same meaning in *girls* as it does in *girlish*, and the morpheme *-ish* has the same meaning in *boyish* as it has in *girlish*.

Intonation

720 In speaking we use **stress, pitch,** and **juncture** to further qualify the meaning of words. Taken together, these comprise **intonation.** Intonation sometimes determines the form class of words and therefore must be taken into account by a writer. A written sentence that may suggest the wrong intonation will be ambiguous; unless punctuation will make it clear, it should be rewritten. Such sentences are rare. But an understanding of the meanings contributed by intonation are important in studying speech. Note the changes in meaning given by shifting the emphasis in the following sentences:

Why don't you sing?

Why *don't* you sing?

Why don't *you* sing?
Why don't you *sing?*

721 STRESS Four degrees of stress (loudness) are usually identified in English. The stress symbols, for softest to loudest, are /ᵕ\^/ʼ/. A sentence may be marked as follows: *Thĕ rédbùd hăd ă rêd búd.* Stress contributes strongly to meaning, as in differentiating *redbud* (the Judas tree) and *red bud* (the bud of a tree which is red in color).

722 PITCH Four levels of pitch are distinguished, marked as follows from lowest to highest: /1/2/3/4/. Pitch may also be marked for a sentence by lines above and below letters, the higher the line, the higher the pitch. The following shows both ways of marking pitch, a strong feeling of exasperation (an emotion) giving a high pitch to *are:*

2— 4 2 3 1—
Where are you going?

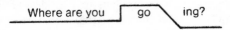

As an ordinary question this sentence might be marked for pitch as follows:

Where are you ⌐go⌐ ing?

723 JUNCTURE There are four junctures (vocal pauses): plus juncture /+/, single-bar juncture /|/, double-bar juncture /‖/, and double-cross juncture /#/.

Plus juncture is the suggestion of a break between phonemes that distinguishes, for instance, between *ice + cream* and *I + scream.* Actually, although the same phonemes are used, there is a slight difference in them. There is usually no actual break or pause in the sound.

Single-bar juncture occurs after a primary (loudest) stress in a sentence if the pitch remains the same: *The girl in the car | is my cousin.*

Double-bar juncture occurs after a primary stress when there is a slight rise in pitch: *Major Hamilton ‖ flying a routine mission ‖ made a remarkable discovery.* This juncture corresponds roughly to the points in a sentence which would be punctuated by commas or, possibly, dashes; but the correspondence is not exact. This juncture may also occur at the end of certain questions.

Double-cross juncture occurs when the pitch falls and the voice trails off into silence: *We lived there ten years # however ‖ I didn't* *like it #.* This juncture frequently corresponds to end punctuation, especially the period, or to the semicolon; but the correspondence is not an exact one.

724 This brief outline of structural linguistics will of course raise many questions that cannot be answered here. One should not assume, however, that such questions cannot be answered. Although much work remains to be done in the field, a great many problems have been thoroughly and satisfactorily worked out. A study of the subject can be highly rewarding, and many of the books listed in the Bibliography at the end of this chapter will be of special value for those interested in the study of linguistics. Most of these books assume a thorough knowledge of conventional grammar.

Transformational/Generative Grammar

725 The basic assumption of this significant new grammar of the linguists is that all the sentences in a language can be derived from "kernel" sentences by means of transformations. These grammars may also be defined as a method of "generating" the sentences of a language, so that you will find the term *generative* grammar as well as *transformational* grammar applied to the systems of language study based on the assumptions implicit in the idea of deriving complex sentence structures from the simplest possible patterns.

There is a distinction between the two terms to be noted, however. In brief, the transformation can be described as an operation or procedure by the use of formulas, and these, by extension, can be developed into ones that generate the grammatical sequences and reject the ungrammatical—the aim or goal of the study of grammar.

Kernel Sentences

726 The basic or kernel sentences of a language are simple declarative sentences with verbs in the active voice. Theoretically, a native speaker of the language will recognize these sentences as grammatically correct, so that more complicated sentences derived from them by strict transformation rules will also be grammatically correct. Negative, passive, and interrogative sentences are all produced by transformation of kernel sentences. So also are sentences with most kinds of adjectival and adverbial modifiers or conjunctions or other connectives. These, of course, include the most sophisticated sentences of the language.

Simple Transformations

727 Students of English are already familiar with the ways in which an active sentence, for example, can be changed to the passive form.

The active sentence must have an object:

He shot a *tiger*.

In the passive, the object becomes the subject:

A *tiger* was shot by him.

The phrase *by him* replaces the subject *he* of the active sentence, but now it is not grammatically necessary:

A tiger was shot.

The description of the language is simplified by being limited basically to a small number of simple sentences of this kind. The transformations that generate all other sentences from these kernel sentences are numerous and varied, but each follows invariable steps, and it is this constancy of the transformations that gives the greatest promise to the generative method.

The Basic Sentence Patterns

728 It will at once be seen that the basic pattern of the kernel sentences is the familiar subject-predicate structure.

	Subject	**Predicate**
Pattern I	Boys	fight.
Pattern II	Boys	play ball.
Pattern III A	Boys	become men.
Pattern III B	Boys	are fighters.
Pattern IV A	Boys	seem brave.
Pattern IV B	Boys	are brave.
Pattern V	Boys	are everywhere.

729 PATTERN I   **N + V**

Pattern I, the simplest pattern, may consist of only a noun and a verb—**N + V**: *Boys argue.* But the noun is often preceded by a noun-determiner: a structure word (715) such as *a, an,* or *the*. The symbol for noun-determiner may be written (**n-d**), the parentheses indicating that the determiner is not always necessary. Every basic pattern has a subject that may be written as (**n-d**) + **N**. But the predicate is different for each pattern: it is what distinguishes the patterns.

The following are examples of Pattern I sentences:

(**n-d**)	+	**N**	+	**V**
		Boys		argue.
The		corn		grows.
		Dogs		bark.

730 PATTERN II $(n\text{-}d)N^1 + V + (n\text{-}d)N^2$

Many verbs require complements and so will not fit into PATTERN I. All the other patterns include complements, which may be nouns, adjectives, or adverbs. PATTERNS II and III require noun complements. These are PATTERN II sentences:

$(n\text{-}d)N^1$	+	V	+	$(n\text{-}d)N^2$
The boys		played		a game.
Jane		likes		music.
Columbus		discovered		America.

The **direct object** is labeled N^2 because it does not represent or refer to the same thing as the subject noun, N^1.

Some verbs can be used in either PATTERN I or PATTERN II. You can say either "The boys played" or "The boys played a game." PATTERN I verbs are used as **intransitive** verbs, and PATTERN II verbs as **transitive** verbs (173–176).

731 PATTERN III

There are always two nouns in PATTERN III linked by verbs such as *become* or *remain* (III A) or forms of *be* (III B). *Be* differs from other words in many ways and therefore sentences with forms of *be* are grouped separately in each pattern.

The symbol for a predicate is **VP** (verb phrase) and the symbol for "is rewritten as" is an arrow: →. The predicate for PATTERN III A is written as $VP \rightarrow V + N^1$: Thus there are two positions (or "slots") in this pattern labeled N^1, because both nouns refer to the same person or thing.

732 PATTERN III A $NP + VP \rightarrow V + N^1$

$(n\text{-}d)N^1$	+	V	+	$(n\text{-}d)N^1$
Boys		become		men.
Jane		became		a salesperson
The team		became		champions.
Joe		remained		a bore.

733 PATTERN III B $NP + VP \rightarrow be + N^1$

$(n\text{-}d)N^1$	+	be	+	$(n\text{-}d)N^1$
Churchill		was		a statesman.
Whales		are		mammals.
Fred		is		a halfback.

734 PATTERN IV

The first three sentence patterns above require only two form classes: noun and verb. PATTERN IV requires an adjective. The verbs used most often in PATTERN IV A are *seem, taste, look, feel, smell, sound, appear, grow, get,* as well as *become* and *remain*. In PATTERN IV B some form of *be* is used.

735 PATTERN **IV A**   NP + VP → V + adj
                   (n-d)N   +   V   +   adj.
                   The boys   got   angry.
                   The sun   grew   hot.
                   The fruit   tastes good.
                   The fur   feels   soft.

736 PATTERN **IV B**   VP → be + adj.
                   (n-d)N   +   be   +   adj.
                   The eggs   were   fresh.
                   The heat   was   uncomfortable.
                   The women   are   brave.

737 PATTERN **V**   NP + VP → be + adv.
This pattern is unusual but important. The adverbs in this pattern are usually adverbs of *place*, but occasionally they are adverbs of *time*.
                   (n-d)N   +   be   +   adv
                   The guests   are   outside.
                   Water   is   everywhere.
                   The meeting   is   tomorrow
                   The planes   were   above.

738 Below is a simple *tree diagram*, a vertical diagrammatic representation of the rules governing a typical Pattern I kernel sentence.

The boy worked.

Key
S = Sentence
NP = Noun Phrase
Det = Determiner (n-d)
N = Noun
VP = Verb Phrase
Aux = Auxiliary
VBX = Verb Expression
Vb$_{non-tran}$ = Verb Nontransitive
V$_{int}$ = Verb Intransitive

These kernel sentences of transformational grammar may seem completely familiar to you. It is, of course, intended that they should be. In this grammar you start with what you already know and largely understand. From these simple basic sentences you can, with strict transformational rules, generate entirely new sentences—as long and as complicated as you wish. And if your kernel sentences are grammatically correct, your transformations will be grammatically correct.

Transformations

739 Scholars who have tried to write complete descriptions of a language have found that a dozen tightly packed volumes were not enough. A language has an almost unlimited diversity in its structures. But quite ordinary persons learn to use their native language in childhood and often to use it with considerable skill. In essence, it would appear that a language structure is not as complicated as it appears to be. Transformational grammar tries to find the fundamental simplicity of a language in a small set of kernel sentences. The transformation rules give us all the rest of the language.

The There Transformation

740 A common type of English sentence begins with the expletive *there* (239):

> *There* is a messenger here.

This of course is a transformation. From what pattern is this sentence derived? You can easily find out by rewording the sentence without *there:*

> A messenger is here.

You can see at once that this is a PATTERN V sentence. What happens in the transformation? Primarily, the verb is put before the subject, a reversal of the characteristic English word order. Is the form of *be* changed in this reversal? Does *there* have number? No, as used here, the word *there* is merely a signal or marker that the normal subject-predicate order of English is being reversed—it is a word without meaning otherwise. (Do not confuse the expletive *there* with the adverb *there* indicating *place*.) The word *is* continues to agree in person and number with its subject *messenger*.

741 In general, the *there* transformation can be derived only from PATTERN V. However, if the predicate is expanded by using the auxiliary *be*, a transformation originating with PATTERN I may sometimes be obtained.

> Several messengers *leave*.
> Several messengers *are leaving*.
> There *are* several messengers *leaving*.

This is an illustration of the way in which specific restrictions must often be placed on a transformation process.

Transformations Requiring Auxiliaries

742 The final *there* transformation illustrates an important characteristic of English word order. Several transformations introduce a reversal into the normal subject-predicate order. If an auxiliary has been introduced into the predicate, only the auxiliary may be placed before the subject (this applies also to a combination of auxiliaries, the verb-phrase, such as *may have been*). Often an auxiliary expansion is obligatory, as in the *there* transformation based on PATTERN V.

The Question Transformations

743   If an ordinary auxiliary (*can, may, shall, will, must, have, be*) or an auxiliary combination has first been used to expand the predicate, the question transformation may be carried out as with *there* and auxiliaries. However, only the first auxiliary is positioned in front of the subject, the main part of the verb following the subject:

Mr. Baron has arrived. → Has Mr. Baron arrived?

Herbert is skating. → Is Herbert skating?

Herbert might have been skating. → Might Herbert have been skating?

But if no regular auxiliary is present, the main verb usually cannot be placed before the subject (although in older English such constructions were possible). We can no longer change *Herbert skates* to *Skates Herbert?* In this situation we use the special word *do* to fill the need:

Does Herbert skate?

Exceptions to the requirement to pre-position an auxiliary for the question transformation are *be* and sometimes *have* when they are used as main verbs.

He has enough. → Has he enough?

It is ready. → Is it ready?

But in sentences such as "He has it.", American English, unlike British English, requires *do* for the question transformation:

Does he have it? (NOT: Has he it?)

The word *do* may also be a main verb, but it too requires the auxiliary *do* for this transformation.

Did he do the work?

The same type of transformation may be used with some questions introduced by the question markers (717) such as *when, where, why*:

Jane has left. → Why has Jane left?

She will come back. → When will she come back?

Fred lives here. → Where does Fred live?

There are other types of questions, but they need not be treated here.

The Negative Transformation

744 The negative tranformation also requires an auxiliary, but the word order is not changed. Add *not* (or its contracted form in *n't*) to the auxiliary or the first word of an auxiliary combination. *Be* and sometimes *have* are also exceptions in this transformation.

> She will come back. → She won't come back.
> Fred lives here. → Fred doesn't live here.
> She is here. → She isn't here.

The necessity for using *do* when no other auxiliary is present, is the same as for a question transformation.

The Passive Transformation

745 Anyone can readily note the difference between the sentences "The woman became an actress" and "The woman read the play." One can also see that the second sentence can be transformed into the passive, but that the first one cannot. We can not say "The actress was become by the woman," but we can say "The play was read by the woman." PATTERN III A sentences can not be transformed into the passive voice, but PATTERN II sentences can be.

Modification Transformations

746 "The man is intelligent" is a basic sentence PATTERN IV B, and "The man screamed" is a PATTERN I sentence. "The intelligent man screamed" is not a basic sentence but is a transformation. It may be derived from the first two kernel sentences:

> The man is intelligent. } The intelligent man screamed.
> The man screamed.

Complex Sentence Transformations

747 There is nothing difficult even in deriving a complex sentence with an adjective clause from simple kernel sentences. The relative clause is derived from a kernel sentence called the *source*.

> SOURCE: It seems valuable. (IV A)   [INPUT]
> CONSUMER: I found a document. (II)
> RESULT: I found a document that seems valuable.   [OUTPUT]
> SOURCE: I bought a watch. (II)   [INPUT]
> CONSUMER: The watch was an heirloom. (III B)
> RESULT: The watch that I bought was an heirloom.   [OUTPUT]

748 The transformations illustrated here are simplified examples of the transformational method. None of the transformational rules are given because to talk clearly about them requires the use of symbols in precise ways. The symbols look very complicated at first, but they greatly simplify the presentation and use of the method. A full explanation is not possible, of course, in this space; but it is hoped that some of the underlying simplicity and power of the transformational method has been suggested.

Bibliography

Grammar, Usage, Linguistics, and the Teaching of English

Allen, Harold B., *et al. New Dimensions in English, Teacher's Annotated Edition.* New York: McCormick-Mathers Publishing Co., 1967.

——, (ed.). *Readings in Applied English Linguistics, Second Edition.* New York: Appleton-Century-Crofts, 1967.

Baugh, Albert C. *A History of the English Language.* New York: Appleton-Century-Crofts, 1957.

Bernstein, Theodore. *The Careful Writer: A Modern Guide to English Usage.* New York: Atheneum Publishers, 1965.

Bryant, Margaret M. (ed.). *Current American Usage.* New York: Funk and Wagnalls Company, 1962.

Chisolm, William S. *The New English.* New York: Funk & Wagnalls Company, 1969.

Chomsky, Noam. *Syntactic Structures.* The Hague: Mouton & Co., 1957.

Follet, Wilson, *et al. Modern American Usage.* New York: Hill & Wang, Inc., 1966.

Fowler, Henry W. *A Dictionary of Modern English Usage, Second Edition* (Sir Ernest Gower). Oxford: Oxford University Press, 1965.

Gleason, H. A., Jr. *Linguistics and English Grammer.* New York: Holt, Rinehart and Winston, Inc., 1965.

Hudspeth, Robert N., and Donald F. Sturtevant. *The World of Language: A Reader in Linguistics.* New York: Van Nostrand Reinhold, 1967.

Jesperson, Otto. *Essentials of English Grammar.* University, Ala.: U. of Alabama Press, 1964.

——. *Language: Its Nature, Development, and Origin.* New York: Norton, 1964.

Lazarus, Arnold, and Wendell Smith. *Glossary of Literature and Composition.* New York: Grosset & Dunlap, Inc., 1973.

Lester, M. *Introductory Transformational Grammar of English.* New York: Holt, Rinehart and Winston, Inc., 1971.

Moulton, William G. *A Linguistic Guide to Language Learning, Second Edition.* New York: Modern Language Association of America, 1970.

Pei, Mario A. *Glossary of Linguistic Terminology.* New York: Columbia University Press, 1966.

Perrin, Porter G. and Jim W. Corder. *Handbook of Current English, Fourth Edition.* Glenview, Ill.: Scott, Foresman and Company, 1976.

Perrin, Porter G. and Wilma R. Ebbitt. *Writer's Guide and Index to English, Fifth Edition.* Glenview, Ill.: Scott, Foresman and Company, 1972.

Roberts, Paul. *English Syntax.* New York: Harcourt Brace Jovanovich, 1964.

Sapir, Edward. *Language: An Introduction to the Study of Speech.* New York: Harcourt Brace Jovanovich, 1955.

Sledd, James. *A Short Introduction to English Grammar.* Glenview, Ill.: Scott, Foresman, and Company, 1959.

Thomas, O. and Kintgen. *Transformational Grammar and The Teacher of English, Second Edition.* New York: Holt, Rinehart and Winston, Inc., 1974.

Dictionaries

The American College Dictionary. New York: Random House, Inc., 1975.

American Heritage Dictionary of the English Language. Boston: Houghton-Mifflin Company, 1976.

Funk & Wagnalls Standard College Dictionary, new updated edition. New York: Funk & Wagnalls Company, 1968.

The Random House Dictionary, College Edition. New York: Random House, Inc., 1973.

The Random House Dictionary of the English Language. New York: Random House, Inc., 1973.

Webster's New Collegiate Dictionary. Springfield: G. & C. Merriam Co., 1975.

Webster's New World Dictionary of the English Language, Second College Edition. New York: Collins-World, 1974.

Webster's Third New International Dictionary. Springfield: G. & C. Merriam Co., 1971.

Index

Numbers refer to the sections of this book.

Quick Reference Chart

		A	B	C	D
Grammar and Usage	**1**	Sentence parts 1-37	Parts of speech 38-52	Nouns 53-127	Pronoun classes 128-140
	2	Pronoun usage 141-169	Verbs 170-215	Verb usage 216-264	Verbals 265-274
	3	Adjectives 275-315	Adverbs 316-340	Prepositions 341-364	Conjunctions 365-386
Sentences	**4**	Sentence structure 387-416	Style and Variety 417-431	Effectiveness 432-436	Improving structure 437-463
Mechanics	**5**	Capitalization 464-485	Period, semicolon, colon 486-494	Comma 495-506	Quotation marks 507-516
	6	Apostrophe 517-521	Dash, parentheses, brackets 522-528	Question mark exclamation mark, hyphen 529-537	Abbreviations, italics, numerals 538-540
Organizing Ideas	**7**	Paragraph writing 541-550	Writing verse 564-576, 694	Planning and outlining 577-581	Business letters 589-615
	8	Social letters 616-624	Newspaper writing 625-632	Research paper 633-639	Oral communication 641-652
Diction	**9**	Classes of words 653-664	Usage Glossary 665-674	Figures of speech 676-682	Spelling and vocabulary 684-696

The letters at the top of the chart and the numbers at the left may be used as a simple code for composition correction. For example, C2 would refer to errors in verb usage.